SEEING GOD'S SMILE
when life is difficult

Pete Beck III

Seeing God's Smile.  Published by Master Press.

© 2011 by Pete Beck III All rights reserved

Cover design by Bonnie Smith. Cover photography by Julia Starr.

Printed in the United States. ALL RIGHTS RESERVED No part of this publication may be reproduced, stored in a retrieval system, or transmitted, in any form or by any other means—electronic, mechanical, photocopying, recording, or otherwise—without written permission

Seeing God's Smile ISBN#: 978-0-9834326-0-9

For information: Master Press, 318 S.E. 3th Terrace, Cape Coral, FL 33990

Scripture quoted by permission.

All scripture quotations, unless otherwise indicated, are taken from the NET Bible® copyright ©1996-2006 by Biblical Studies Press, L.L.C. www.bible.org. All rights reserved. This material is available in its entirety as a free download or online web use at http://www.netbible.org.

Scripture quotations marked (ESV) are from The Holy Bible, English Standard Version® (ESV®), copyright © 2001 by Crossway, a publishing ministry of Good News Publishers. Used by permission. All rights reserved.

Scripture quotations marked (The Message) are from The Message. Copyright © 1993, 1994, 1995, 1996, 2000, 2001, 2002. Used by permission of NavPress Publishing Group.

Scripture quotations marked (NIV) are from the HOLY BIBLE, NEW INTERNATIONAL VERSION®. Copyright © 1973, 1978, 1984 Biblica. Used by permission of Zondervan. All rights reserved.

CONTENTS

Thanks...7
Foreword..9
Out of the Shadows..13
Not if, but when..20
Life Is a Journey...23
Going Where We Don't Want to Go..27
Wrestling with the Angel...31
Seeing God's Smile..37
A Quick Review..41
We Are Never Alone..43
The Lord Is My Keeper...46
Taking the Sting Out of Death...50
Rejecting Rejection..54
Surrender, Unconditional Peace, and the Secret Place............58
Unconditional Praise - The Gateway to Overcoming Faith........63
Grace is for the "Whats", Not the "What Ifs"........................66
The Only Safe Place Is the Secret Place 69
Reassessing Priorities and Paying Vows 72
God's Gym..75
Everything Is Against Me!?..78
The Gold Standard..80
Out of Control..82
Living on "Borrowed Time"..84
Snatch Proof...87
The Good Shepherd and the Secret Place..............................93
Our Last Chance...96
The Greatest Thing and Our Final Destination......................100

THANKS

I owe a special debt of gratitude to those who have helped with this book. I thank my Mom, Jane Beck, my son, Clark, Carolyn Gibbs, Skip Anderson, and Bonnie Smith who each contributed by reviewing the text and making editorial suggestions. My appreciation also goes to Bonnie Smith who did a beautiful job designing the book cover and formatting the text. Thanks to many others who encouraged me to write this book, especially my wife, Martha, who introduced me to Jesus and whose love, encouragement, and friendship have been unwavering.

But thanks most of all to the Lord, who is my forever Friend and Keeper and who continues to reveal His amazing love every day.

FOREWORD

"Do not let your hearts be distressed.
You believe in God; believe also in me.
2 There are many dwelling places in my Father's house.
Otherwise, I would have told you,
because I am going away to make ready a place for you.
3 And if I go and make ready a place for you,
I will come again and take you to be with me,
so that where I am you may be too.
4 And you know the way where I am going."
5 Thomas said, "Lord, we don't know where you are going.
How can we know the way?"
6 Jesus replied, "I am the way, and the truth, and the life.
No one comes to the Father except through me.
John 14:1-6

LIFE IS A JOURNEY from the alienation from God and others, and the bondage produced by sin, back to the heart and presence of our Heavenly Father. Jesus left the glorious bliss of being in His Father's presence to come to this sin blasted earth on a rescue mission. He lived about thirty-three years, three of those in public ministry. He fearlessly testified of His Father's love and holiness and offered a way to be reconciled with Him. He took on the religious power brokers of His day as a way to demonstrate that the gospel is not about religious performance. Instead, the good news about Christ is that He offers a totally new and unexpected way of being in right standing with God. He is the Way, the Truth, and the Life. It is only through trusting in Him - His finished work of redemption, His glorious resurrection, and the indwelling presence and power of His Holy Spirit - that people can experience true life that never ends.

But even after we come to believe in what Jesus did for us, receive by faith all the benefits, and begin to enjoy the incomparable privilege of fellowship with God, there remains much work to be done in our souls. Deeply ingrained lies die hard and so does our unbelief. It is difficult for us to let go of the things we fear and the things in which we trust that are God supplanters. By clinging to false hopes and false beliefs, we sabotage the Lord's work of revealing Himself more fully to us. That being the case, God has to bring us through situations and difficulties that serve to destroy our false hopes and shatter lying illusions. The end result is a revelation of God that is worth whatever it takes to get it, but as we are going through the fires of testing and discipline, we may feel as if God is trying to kill us.

This should not surprise us, since Jesus warned us that if we seek to hold on to our lives, we will lose them. It is only as we cast ourselves completely upon the Lord's love and mercy that we discover that by giving our lives away, we get them back again.

God has placed each of us on a path, a journey, called life. He has carefully planned a course for us to travel that will give us opportunities to leave behind our false gods and bondage inducing lies. If we will turn to the Lord in the midst of life's tests and difficulties, God will see to it that we get to know Christ in His many wonderful roles. He is the Way, the Truth, the Life, the Resurrection, the Good Shepherd, our Righteousness, our Keeper, our Victory Banner - and the list goes on.

The journey called life provides the means to this end. It is only by taking the journey that we can arrive where God wants us to be. Some people want to get to the destination without ever making the journey, which is impossible. They just want to snap their fingers and be there. It doesn't work that way. Some want to take the journey, but don't want to let God draw the map or choose the path. If left to us, we would calculate how to avoid all the hard places, but God has selected a particular course for each of us that will individually and perfectly suit our need to know Christ better.

> *Therefore, since we are surrounded by such a great cloud of witnesses,*
> *we must get rid of every weight and the sin that clings so closely,*
> *and run with endurance the race set out for us,*
> *2 keeping our eyes fixed on Jesus,*

> *the pioneer and perfecter of our faith.*
> *For the joy set out for him he endured the cross,*
> *disregarding its shame, and has taken his seat*
> *at the right hand of the throne of God.*
> *Hebrews 12:1-2*

The course God has set for each of us will not be easy, and will require great endurance to finish.

> *For this reason we also, from the day we heard about you,*
> *have not ceased praying for you and asking God*
> *to fill you with the knowledge of his will*
> *in all spiritual wisdom and understanding,*
> *10 so that you may live worthily of the Lord*
> *and please him in all respects —*
> *bearing fruit in every good deed,*
> *growing in the knowledge of God,*
> *11 being strengthened with all power*
> *according to his glorious might*
> *for the display of all patience and steadfastness,*
> *joyfully 12 giving thanks to the Father who has qualified you*
> *to share in the saints' inheritance in the light.*
> *Colossians 1:9-12*

God works in our hearts and lives as we make the journey and face all sorts of difficulties, tests, and trials. The grace of God will see us through to the end, and God will sovereignly work out everything for our good, if we place our trust in the One called the Way, Jesus.

When we meet up with life's challenges, instead of viewing them as enemies or unwelcome intruders, we can adopt another view – seeing them as opportunities to get to know God in a brand new or deeper way. If we turn to God in the face of hardship, fear, or whatever tests us, we will find that his love is unfailing, his wisdom incomparable, and his power sovereign. The purpose of this book is to help you understand some of the ways God uses the difficulties of life to reveal Himself more fully to us. When this happens, we will be able to see His smile despite anything else that looms against us. We will experience the victory of a faith that is grounded in the surety of God's love and faithfulness. This is a key to living in joy, peace and victory.

I hope you will allow me to share some of my journey with you as you read this book. If I am able to communicate to you what God has shared with me, I don't think you will be disappointed, and I believe what is contained in these pages will be an encouragement to you as you make your own journey with God.

OUT OF THE SHADOWS

*For this reason we also, from the day we heard about you,
have not ceased praying for you and asking God
to fill you with the knowledge of his will
in all spiritual wisdom and understanding,
10 so that you may live worthily of the Lord
and please him in all respects —
bearing fruit in every good deed,
growing in the knowledge of God,
11 being strengthened with all power according to his glorious might
for the display of all patience and steadfastness,
joyfully 12 giving thanks to the Father who has qualified you
to share in the saints' inheritance in the light.
Colossians 1:9-12*

LIFE IS FILLED WITH SHADOWS. Light and darkness are part of our world. Darkness has always been associated with fear, evil, and the unknown. Shadows are caused when light is partially obscured by some object. The larger the shadow, the greater is that which casts it. Death has long cast its eerie and ominous shadow across the entire human race. It hangs over all people like a shroud. Into this shadowland, God sent his only begotten Son.

*...the people who sit in darkness have seen a great light,
and on those who sit in the region and shadow of death
a light has dawned.
Matthew 4:16*

King David, who knew God intimately, wrote the now famous lines from Psalm 23:

SEEING GOD'S SMILE | 13

> *Even when I must walk through the darkest valley,*
> *I fear no danger, for you are with me;*
> *your rod and your staff reassure me.*
> *Psalms 23:4*

In the above verse, the word translated "darkest valley" in the Hebrew means "deep shadow." The fear of death can cast a shadow of fear, hopelessness, judgment, and bondage. Some translators use the phrase "the valley of the shadow of death." Death's shadow is the place from which every person begins his or her journey because of sin. Before Christ came, no one had any hope of escape. Then the Light of the World came to save us and lead us to freedom and into a new kingdom bathed in the glorious radiance of God's presence.

The phrase "the valley of the shadow of death" suggests that people see death as something huge - a mountain of fear, which casts a big shadow. For many, death is an ever present foe, always looming in the background of our thoughts, always waiting for us at the end of our days, always a specter as portrayed by the caricature called the Grim Reaper. Jesus journeyed into that shadowland in order to procure our release from death's powerful grip. He defeated death so we can come into the light of eternal life.

> *Therefore, since the children share in flesh and blood,*
> *he likewise shared in their humanity, so that through death*
> *he could destroy the one who holds the power of death*
> *(that is, the devil), 15 and set free those who were*
> *held in slavery all their lives by their fear of death.*
> *Hebrews 2:14-15*

But shadows are not all bad. There is another shadow that is a place of refuge - the shadow of the Almighty.

> *As for you, the one who lives*
> *in the shelter of the sovereign One,*
> *and resides in the protective shadow of the mighty king —*
> *2 I say this about the LORD,*
> *my shelter and my stronghold, my God in whom I trust —*
> *3 he will certainly rescue you*

> *from the snare of the hunter and from the destructive plague.*
> *4 He will shelter you with his wings;*
> *you will find safety under his wings.*
> *His faithfulness is like a shield or a protective wall.*
> *Psalms 91:1-4*

Once again, here the idea behind the shadow is that God is huge and, in this case, casts a protective shadow, not a gloomy one. This is a shadow that is well lit with God's presence but still hides us from the adversary and the storms of life. God's shadow is a hiding place, a refuge.

James tells us that there is no "shadow of turning" in God.

> *All generous giving and every perfect gift is from above,*
> *coming down from the Father of lights,*
> *with whom there is no variation or the slightest hint of change.*
> *James 1:17*

This means that, unlike the shadows cast by the sun which are constantly moving, God's protective shadow never shifts. He is absolutely truthful. His promises can be fully trusted because His character is a giant rock of faithfulness.

Life is meant to be a journey out from under the shadow of death and into the shadow of the Almighty. Jesus, the Light of the World, delivers from death those who trust in Him and introduces them to His Abba, the Father of Lights, who places us under His protective shadow. Have you believed on the Lord Jesus and let Him take you by the hand to lead you out from under fear and into safety? Have you begun the journey? There is no time like today!

Sadly, many prefer darkness over light.

> *Now this is the basis for judging:*
> *that the light has come into the world*
> *and people loved the darkness rather than the light,*
> *because their deeds were evil.*
> *20 For everyone who does evil deeds hates the light*
> *and does not come to the light, so that their deeds will not be exposed.*

> *21 But the one who practices the truth comes to the light,*
> *so that it may be plainly evident that his deeds have been done in God.*
> *John 3:19-21*

Light haters would rather live in a place where their sinful deeds and thoughts remain undisclosed, at least for now. They choose to live without regard for God, refusing to submit their lives to the One Who is the Life. For these, there is no hope, unless they one day see the error of their ways and turn to God. But for those who are willing to come into God's light by acknowledging their sin and trusting in the good news about Christ, God transfers them out from under the shadow of the lord of death and into the gloriously bright kingdom of the Son of God.

Those who long to be free from the clawing arms of the shadow of death need only cry out to the Light of the World. If you seek Him with all your heart, you will find Him. If you ask Him to come into your life, He has promised that He will never cast you aside.

> *Everyone whom the Father gives me will come to me,*
> *and the one who comes to me I will never send away.*
> *John 6:37*

That's a promise from God, with Whom there is no trace of shiftiness or falsehood.

But, so much for the general introduction: let's get right to the point. Yes, life is a journey, and God is the One who maps our course. Not one of us creatures gets to choose where that journey begins or ends. None of us can foresee or prepare for all that will come our way over a lifetime.

Some people seem so incredibly blessed, while others suffer extraordinarily. Why is this? Is there anything good that can come from our suffering? People have wrestled with the meaning of life for millennia, and when something unexpectedly threatens to cut our life span short or significantly diminish its quality, we are driven to ponder some very deep things. Why did this happen to me? Where is God in all this? Is He even there? Is He really in charge of everything that takes place in my life? What will happen to me now? Will I survive this? Is there any ultimate meaning to life? Shadows of doubt and despair can invade our lives, casting gloominess over everything.

Many people go through life with a fear of sickness, death, and the unknown. Cancer, the "Big C," lurks quietly and ominously, threatening to randomly intrude into our lives and thrust its terrifying face into our consciousness, forcing us to confront fear and the shadow of death, something we would rather put off indefinitely or ignore all together.

This was the way it was for me when I first faced the possibility that I might have cancer in 2005. God brought things to the surface in my life because He was ready to help me deal with them. Often that which we fear, instead of being something horrible and debilitating, actually serves as a gateway for God to bring healing, deliverance and freedom.

Jesus conquered death by going through it and confronting it head on. His victory over death and the grave via the cross and His subsequent resurrection set all believers free from God's judgment; but, until we experience that freedom for ourselves, it tends to be just a theological truth. God wants His declared truth to become our experienced truth. For this to happen we must sometimes go through that which we fear so we can discover the reality of God's victory.

When we find ourselves cornered by something we fear or otherwise would not choose to go through, we may feel as David did when he penned these words in the Psalms.

> *My heart beats violently within me;*
> *the horrors of death overcome me.*
> *5 Fear and panic overpower me; terror overwhelms me.*
> *6 I say, "I wish I had wings like a dove!*
> *I would fly away and settle in a safe place!*
> *7 Look, I will escape to a distant place;*
> *I will stay in the wilderness. (Selah)*
> *8 I will hurry off to a place that is safe*
> *from the strong wind and the gale."*
> *Psalms 55:4-8*

But God did not allow David to simply escape from his difficulties.

Instead he had to go through many trying experiences on his journey through life, as we must also.

> *They strengthened the souls of the disciples*
> *and encouraged them to continue in the faith, saying,*
> *"We must enter the kingdom of God through many persecutions*
> *[Greek: thlipsis – pressures, afflictions, trials, persecutions]."*
> *Acts 14:22*

We experience freedom and victory in Christ by learning that His grace is sufficient to carry us through any and every trial. Very few of us would choose this route to victory; so, God, in His wisdom, may choose it for us. That is what He did for me.

This book was written after my bout with prostate cancer in order to share with you what God ministered to me in the hope that you will experience the same blessing as I, and even more so. Instead of adversity tearing you down, you will find that God's grace will be there to make you stronger. Faith is like a muscle that must be exercised in order to grow. Your test can become a launching pad into a journey from fear to faith, from anxiety to peace, and from sadness to joy.

When we encounter our fears head on, God will surprise us with what He teaches us about Himself, His grace, and about life in general. The difficulties we go through will show us the real condition of our faith and our hearts so we can make the necessary adjustments to align ourselves with God's heart and His will for our lives.

When we confront our fears, it forces us to make a journey to the secret place of God's presence, the refuge of the shadow of the Almighty. It is a place hidden from life's storms and the threats of the enemy. It is a place where God's peace and presence reign undisturbed. You too have access to this secret place when you surrender unconditionally to God's will for your life and trust in His love for you and His power to make all things ultimately work together for your good. God will assist you to become a true believer – someone who has victorious, overcoming faith in the middle of the storm.

Our prayer will be like King David's:

Protect me as you would protect the pupil of your eye!
Hide me in the shadow of your wings!
Psalms 17:8

NOT IF, BUT WHEN

*I have told you these things so that in me you may have peace.
In the world you have trouble and suffering,
but take courage —
I have conquered the world."*
John 16:33

TRIALS AND TRIBULATIONS ARE NOT OPTIONAL. They are part of God's plan to transform us and to give us the opportunity to develop overcoming faith. Surprised? We should not be. Just consider how much bad "stuff" happens to even good people. The book of Job addresses this question head on and comes up with the disconcerting answer that God Himself was indirectly behind Job's suffering, using it to take Job to a brand new level of faith and knowledge of God's ways and Person.

Suffering is a normal and necessary part of life, without which we cannot reach maturity in the Lord. Stop right here. Did you really grasp what you just read? Suffering is absolutely necessary if we want to grow in God! Some of us may be wondering if that is even scriptural. Is that the truth? As much as we would like it to be otherwise, that is the "gospel truth". Paul wrote:

*And if children, then heirs (namely, heirs of God
and also fellow heirs with Christ) — if indeed we suffer with him
so we may also be glorified with him.
18 For I consider that our present sufferings cannot even be
compared to the glory that will be revealed to us.*
Romans 8:17-18

When things seem to be going our way, living "by faith" can seem easy or even unnecessary. We can begin to believe that we will never waver or have to suffer through a severe trial. King David expressed this point of view when he penned:

> *He says to himself, "I will never be upended,*
> *because I experience no calamity."*
> Psalms 10:6

In fact, some Christians even have developed an unbiblical theology which more or less says that if we have enough faith, we can stave off bad things from happening to us. But this does not line up with what Jesus taught. In fact, the Bible warns us that in this life we will encounter many pressures, tribulations and trials. Refer to this chapter's opening verse, for example.

We can avoid the consequences of personal sin by obeying God, but all of us are caught in a vortex of reaping and sowing that has enveloped the entire human race. We often get "slammed" by others reaping the consequences for their sin. No one lives in a vacuum. Have you ever said, "I am not afraid to drive on snow, but I am afraid of the other drivers and what they might do to me." You get my "drift"? (Sorry to lamely continue the snow analogy.) We can live wisely and seek to serve God with all our hearts, but that does not insulate us from trouble and tests and pressures and persecutions. No man is an island. We are all connected in the fabric of life and affected by what others do or do not do.

Paul as an apostle was used by God to lay sound doctrinal foundations. He wanted to make sure that the people he cared for would be able to stand in the face of adversity. He did not want them to be caught unaware. So he wrote:

> *We sent Timothy, our brother and fellow worker for God*
> *in the gospel of Christ, to strengthen you*
> *and encourage you about your faith,*
> *3 so that no one would be shaken by these afflictions.*
> *For you yourselves know that we are destined for this.*
> 1 Thessalonians 3:2-3

God allows suffering in our lives for any number of reasons, but chiefly that we may bring glory to God and grow in our faith and knowledge of Him. In Matthew chapter seven, Jesus warned us to build our "house", our lives, upon the rock of obedience to His Word so that when the storms of life come our way, we will be able to stand. It was understood that everyone will have to endure some storms. It is not "if" they will come, but "when."

If we do not expect to encounter difficulties and challenges in our lives, we will likely be ill prepared to weather them. However, if we know they are coming, we can prepare and "steel" ourselves to courageously meet the challenge by faith. We must believe that God's grace will be sufficient when we need it. His grace is not to help us squeak by and somehow survive; rather, it transforms us into overcomers.

Paul wrote:

*No, in all these things we have complete victory
through him who loved us!
Romans 8:37*

I encourage you to expect great things from God. If you picked up this book because you are in the middle of some difficulty and are feeling desperate or maybe even hopeless, take courage. What you are going through will work out for your good and God's glory! What the devil means for evil, God intends for good.

*As for you, you meant to harm me,
but God intended it for a good purpose,
so he could preserve the lives of many people,
as you can see this day.
Genesis 50:20*

LIFE IS A JOURNEY

*Thomas said, "Lord, we don't know where you are going.
How can we know the way?"
6 Jesus replied, "I am the way, and the truth, and the life.
No one comes to the Father except through me.
John 14:5-6*

HOW WE VIEW THE PURPOSE OF LIFE will make a great difference in how we experience it. Jesus is the Way, and through Him all of life is a journey to know God the Father. Jesus told His disciples that He was excited about leaving planet earth to return to Abba, which was the familiar name by which He addressed His heavenly Father. Our modern equivalent would be something like "Daddy." One of the greatest revelations Jesus gave to us is that believers can approach the awesome God of the universe as a small child comes to her Daddy. Just as a young one will run into the arms of his Daddy after a long separation, Jesus was ready to be rejoined with His Abba in heaven, after around thirty-three years of a type of separation during which He accomplished His earthly ministry.

*Peace I leave with you; my peace I give to you;
I do not give it to you as the world does.
Do not let your hearts be distressed or lacking in courage.
28 You heard me say to you,
'I am going away and I am coming back to you.'
If you loved me, you would be glad
that I am going to the Father,
because the Father is greater than I am.
John 14:27-28*

Jesus left the joys of being in the glorious brilliance of Abba's presence to come to the shadowland called earth for our sake. His earthly life required Him to take human form and travel into Satan's territory, something that ultimately took Him through the cross, death, and resurrection and then back to His Father in heaven. Our journey through life and its tribulations and joys will lead us ultimately to that same reunion in heaven. But even before we transition to heavenly existence, Christ's victory makes it possible to enjoy life from a whole new perspective here on earth. Instead of being victims, God has made us victors in Christ. No longer should we believers be slaves of dread. He has made it possible for us to rejoice in all things, even hardships and suffering!

The purpose of our existence here on earth is to know, love, and serve God and to bring glory to His name, while boldly proclaiming the good news of the gospel to those who are not yet part of the eternal family. Paul, one of the early church's greatest leaders who wrote much of the New Testament, informs us that God is also actively transforming us so that we may come to resemble our Lord.

> *And we know that all things work together for good for those*
> *who love God, who are called according to his purpose,*
> *29 because those whom he foreknew he also predestined*
> *to be conformed to the image of his Son, that his Son would be the*
> *firstborn among many brothers and sisters.*
> Romans 8:28-29

Putting all of this together, we can say that life is a journey out from under the shadow of death back to the Father as we are transformed into Christ's image. Everything we encounter in life is designed to serve these two purposes, which will bring great glory to God. God will be glorified both by rescuing and transforming us. Hallelujah!

In addition to understanding the above, for us to properly walk the path of the righteous, we must believe some other important Biblical truths. The first one is that God is in control or is sovereign. This doctrine is a cornerstone upon which a stable Christian life is built. This means that God is loving, powerful, and wise and ultimately works out things for His ends.

> *All the inhabitants of the earth are regarded as nothing.*
> *He does as he wishes with the army of heaven*
> *and with those who inhabit the earth.*
> *No one slaps his hand and says to him,*
> *'What have you done?'*
> *Daniel 4:35*

Secondly, we must believe that God is working all things together for our good and for His glory. This means that God sovereignly requires everything that befalls us to work to these two ends. This also means that the worst thing the devil may do to us has to ultimately work for our good! Please don't quickly read this and go on without deeply considering what this means. This is extremely good news and is foundational for developing overcoming faith.

> *And we know that all things work together for good*
> *for those who love God, who are called according to his purpose.*
> *Romans 8:28*

> *For all these things are for your sake,*
> *so that the grace that is including more and more people may cause*
> *thanksgiving to increase to the glory of God.*
> *2 Corinthians 4:15*

The third truth we must believe and put into practice is that it is proper and necessary to praise God in all things. This is a scriptural principle that follows logically from the first two points. If God is sovereign, and if He is working all things together for my good and His glory, then I should and must praise Him in all things.

> *Always rejoice, 17 constantly pray,*
> *18 in everything give thanks.*
> *For this is God's will for you in Christ Jesus.*
> *1 Thessalonians 5:16-18*

> *giving thanks always and for everything to God the Father*
> *in the name of our Lord Jesus Christ,*
> *Ephesians 5:20 (ESV)*

If we put these three truths into practice in our lives, we will be able to sail through difficulties because we will be in a continual attitude of faith and a posture of praise. This is not some "pie in the sky" theory. It really works because it is based on truth, and God's grace will always be there to help us. If we choose to do otherwise, we will find ourselves among the doubters and complainers who are overthrown when adversity comes along. We will be like the person who built his house on the sand, whose ability to stand firm was quickly eroded, resulting in disaster. Our faith does not remove the difficulties and tests; rather, it gives us God's victory of faith in the middle of them.

So then, life is a journey that must be travelled by faith in a sovereign, loving, and wise God.

> *And he is also the father of the circumcised,*
> *who are not only circumcised, but who also walk*
> *in the footsteps of the faith that our father Abraham possessed*
> *when he was still uncircumcised.*
> Romans 4:12

Life is a journey through adversity and tribulations that God uses to transform us into Christ's image and increase our revelation of and faith in Him. Life is a journey that is meant to be joyful, despite its ups and downs. For those who learn to trust and praise God in all things, the path just keeps getting brighter and brighter as we get closer and closer to our reunion with Abba. God wants to move us from the shadowland of doubt and fear into the bright light of childlike faith in Him.

> *But the path of the righteous is like the bright morning light,*
> *growing brighter and brighter until full day.*
> Proverbs 4:18

GOING WHERE WE DON'T WANT TO GO

"I tell you the solemn truth, when you were young, you tied your clothes around you and went wherever you wanted, but when you are old, you will stretch out your hands, and others will tie you up and bring you where you do not want to go." 19 (Now Jesus said this to indicate clearly by what kind of death Peter was going to glorify God.) After he said this, Jesus told Peter, "Follow me."
John 21:18-19

FOR MOST OF US, our lives become gradually more constricted as we grow older. God begins narrowing the path leading towards the final gate that will give us passage from this life to the next. When we are young, life seems like a boundless adventure, full of unlimited possibilities. As we age, we begin to better understand our own limitations and those imposed on us by what is sometimes a very unfair world. In some cases, we have very little "wiggle room" because of reaping the consequences of unwise decisions made long ago. We may be limited by finances, lack of education, or additional family responsibilities. Old age usually brings with it diminished physical and mental capabilities, which further hedge us in. We cannot do all the things we once did, even if we still wanted to do so. This process is usually slow but inexorable. When we wake up one day to its accumulated effect, we may find ourselves up to our eyeballs in what some call a "midlife crisis." What has my life amounted to? How shall I live out the rest of my days? For some this is exciting, but for others it is quite depressing.

In contrast to the slow process of aging, for some the path may narrow unexpectedly when confronted by life-threatening or life-altering situations from which there is no escape. Men and women who are summoned to war have this kind of experience. For me, this happened when I received a diagnosis of prostate cancer in March of 2007. Nobody wants to have cancer, and especially not a life-threatening version. Up until that time, God had preserved me from having to face my mortality so seriously, but at that point I had to meet the challenge. There was no getting out of it.

My PSA (prostate specific antigen) number had jumped substantially in six months. This sudden increase caused me great concern. I now had to deal with the possibility that I most likely had cancer and that it might have even metastasized, which, apart from a miracle, is a death sentence. However, my doctor did tell me that he believed we had caught it early enough so that it would not be life threatening. We had to "prove" that prognosis by doing a CT scan and later a biopsy of the lymph nodes following their surgical removal. I believe God arranged things so that I would not lightly approach this or easily shrug it off. I had to look death square in the eye and find out if God's grace was indeed sufficient, as I had preached for many years.

When God determines that we will go through something, there is no use trying to squirm out of it. I felt trapped, but it was a good thing; although, it was nothing I would have chosen. I was being forced to take steps I did not want to take and deal with things I did not wish to confront. But God has plans of which we are not always aware. Sometimes they run counter to what we would choose for ourselves. The Bible tells us this:

A person plans his course, but the LORD directs his steps.
Proverbs 16:9

Indeed, my plans are not like your plans,
and my deeds are not like your deeds,
9 for just as the sky is higher than the earth, so my deeds are
superior to your deeds and my plans superior to your plans.
Isaiah 55:8-9

Life is a mystery. We consider ourselves to be rational (usually) and accountable (sometimes) beings who are required to make choices every day, but God is directing our steps and lives in ways we sometimes fail to discern, understand, or appreciate. It is important to remember that God is sovereign and is working all things together for our good and His glory. As we will see, this is a foundational truth that will be repeated over and over again. It is a great source of overcoming faith and has the ability to lead us to the joy of being hidden in God's secret place.

When God forces us to confront something we fear or to go through a severe trial we would rather avoid, we must become convinced that it will work for our good and His glory.

> *For our momentary, light suffering is producing for us*
> *an eternal weight of glory far beyond all comparison*
> *18 because we are not looking at what can be seen*
> *but at what cannot be seen.*
> *For what can be seen is temporary,*
> *but what cannot be seen is eternal.*
> *2 Corinthians 4:17-18*

Jesus told us that the way of God is narrow and there are few who take it. I believe one reason for this is that God's path to glory requires that we suffer.

> *For all who are led by the Spirit of God are the sons of God.*
> *15 For you did not receive the spirit of slavery leading again to fear,*
> *but you received the Spirit of adoption,*
> *by whom we cry, "Abba, Father."*
> *16 The Spirit himself bears witness to our spirit*
> *that we are God's children.*
> *17 And if children, then heirs (namely, heirs of God and also*
> *fellow heirs with Christ) — if indeed we suffer with him*
> *so we may also be glorified with him*
> *18 For I consider that our present sufferings cannot even be*
> *compared to the glory that will be revealed to us.*
> *Romans 8:14-18*

When we choose to trust God when everything seems to be falling apart, it is painful. None of us want to go the way of suffering, but when we encounter it, we should not be surprised. Rather we should view it as it truly is – an opportunity to share in God's glory. Our faith in God's faithfulness is crucial to our experiencing this good outcome.

> *...everyone who has been fathered by God conquers the world.*
> *This is the conquering power that has conquered the world:*
> *our faith.*
> *1 John 5:4*

Do not fear what you must face. Instead, regard it as an opportunity to grow in faith and character.

> *My brothers and sisters,*
> *consider it nothing but joy when you fall into all sorts of trials,*
> *3 because you know that the testing of your faith produces endurance.*
> *4 And let endurance have its perfect effect, so that you*
> *will be perfect and complete, not deficient in anything.*
> *James 1:2-4*

We should ask God to help us so that our way of handling our test will bring glory to God and give strength to others. Other people are always watching to see if we really trust God or not. Let's not give them a chance to reject the gospel because they don't see it working in our lives. Instead they should be able to see the power of God's grace at work in regular people going through difficult times. How you handle your test may be the key to another person coming to saving faith in Christ. What a privilege!

> *My confident hope is that I will in no way be ashamed*
> *but that with complete boldness, even now as always,*
> *Christ will be exalted in my body, whether I live or die.*
> *Philippians 1:20*

WRESTLING WITH THE ANGEL

He struggled with an angel and prevailed;
he wept and begged for his favor.
He found God at Bethel, and there he spoke with him!
Hosea 12:4

IF GOD ALLOWS A SEVERE TRIAL TO COME into our lives, we must settle it in our hearts that He has a good reason. The Bible says:

For he is not predisposed to afflict or to grieve people.
Lamentations 3:33

This brings you great joy, although you may have to suffer
for a short time in various trials.
1 Peter 1:6

It was good for me to suffer, so that I might learn your statutes.
Psalms 119:71

Instead of fighting Him, as Jacob did, why not simply surrender to His plan and purpose? After struggling all night in a futile battle against the Lord, which human beings can never win, Jacob surrendered, too. The cross has been called the intersection or crossing of our will by God's. The cross symbolizes the death of our will and our desire to determine our own course or direction in life. God's will is usually attractive to us on a deep spiritual level, but the journey toward its fulfillment usually runs counter to what we want. We inevitably encounter the cross when we embrace God's divine purpose. We may struggle fiercely, but we cannot win against God. So why not be wise and surrender early on?

Jacob surrendered with one proviso which we should also adopt: he requested a blessing.

> *Then the man said, "Let me go, for the dawn is breaking."*
> *"I will not let you go," Jacob replied, "unless you bless me."*
> *Genesis 32:26*

As we face the trial before us, we should tell God that we surrender to His will and purpose for our lives in the trial (as best we can) and that we want the blessing contained in it. The old saying that every dark cloud has a silver lining is certainly true with God. There is nothing that the devil and life can throw at us that will not ultimately work for our good. Therefore, we can face everything with the bold confidence of a predestined conqueror. In Christ the battle has already been won.

> *No, in all these things we have complete victory*
> *through him who loved us!*
> *38 For I am convinced that neither death, nor life, nor angels,*
> *nor heavenly rulers, nor things that are present,*
> *nor things to come, nor powers, 39 nor height, nor depth,*
> *nor anything else in creation*
> *will be able to separate us from the love of God*
> *in Christ Jesus our Lord.*
> *Romans 8:37-39*

Adversity presents us with an opportunity to meet God in a fresh new way. Of course, for the Christian, the Lord is always present, but often we neglect to profit from this most amazing gift until pressed into a corner. We humans are so oriented toward self-sufficiency that we often forget about God, for all practical purposes, until we are faced with something so beyond our capacity to cope that we are forced to come running to Him. God is so loving and humble of heart that He accepts us even when we come with such questionable motives.

> *Come to me, all you who are weary and burdened,*
> *and I will give you rest.*
> *29 Take my yoke on you and learn from me,*
> *because I am gentle and humble in heart,*
> *and you will find rest for your souls.*
> *30 For my yoke is easy to bear,*
> *and my load is not hard to carry."*
> *Matthew 11:28-30*

God has no illusions about us, but loves us anyway.

In addition to being an opportunity to meet God in a fresh new way, a severe trial is also an opportunity to hear God's voice in a way that inspires faith. God can and will speak to us through Scripture, other human beings, our circumstances, or simply by communicating directly with our hearts. In my case, the night before getting the results of my CT scan and bone scan, I experienced some anxiety. In the midst of that, I asked God to speak something to my heart that would bring me peace and serve as an anchor for my soul.

> *In the same way God wanted to demonstrate more clearly*
> *to the heirs of the promise that his purpose was unchangeable,*
> *and so he intervened with an oath, 18 so that we who have found*
> *refuge in him may find strong encouragement to hold fast to the hope*
> *set before us through two unchangeable things,*
> *since it is impossible for God to lie. 19 We have this hope as an*
> *anchor for the soul, sure and steadfast, which reaches inside behind the*
> *curtain, 20 where Jesus our forerunner entered on our behalf, since he*
> *became a priest forever in the order of Melchizedek.*
> *Hebrews 6:17-20*

I opened my Bible to a passage that came to my mind, and near it was another passage that seemed to literally "jump off the page." In other words, the Holy Spirit caused me to see something in that passage that I otherwise may have missed. The printed words became "alive" in a way that was personal and inspired faith in my heart. I knew it was God speaking to me.

It came from Psalm 116.

> *Rest once more, my soul, for the LORD has vindicated you.*
> *8 Yes, LORD, you rescued my life from death,*
> *and kept my feet from stumbling.*
> *9 I will serve the LORD in the land of the living.*
> *Psalms 116:7-9*

I knew that God was telling me not to worry because He had delivered my soul from death. God knew what the outcome would be and asked me to trust Him as I awaited the results of the test. How did I know this passage was a personal word from God for me? I cannot tell you, except that I simply knew it. Some people call this experience "knowing in our knower." The spirit within us has the ability to know things intuitively. The Holy Spirit communicates directly with our spirits in a way that sometimes defies a logical explanation. When this happens, however, what the Spirit teaches us will always agree with the written Word of God.

> *But when he, the Spirit of truth, comes,*
> *he will guide you into all truth.*
> *For he will not speak on his own authority,*
> *but will speak whatever he hears,*
> *and will tell you what is to come.*
> *John 16:13*

A similar thing happened when I was "born again" in 1971. After hearing the gospel and learning that Jesus Christ can be known personally, I asked Jesus, if He were real and still alive, to come into my heart and reveal Himself to me. For me it was an experiment, but I was serious and not playing games with God. For God it was an open door. When we crack the door of our hearts open just a little, God will take advantage of it. When I prayed that prayer, Jesus, Who is indeed still alive and perfectly able to communicate with people, actually set up His residence in my heart. My life changed immediately in some noticeable ways. I became happier and more willing to serve other people, but I did not immediately "connect the dots." I made no correlation between that prayer and the inner change that resulted. In fact, I actually forgot for a while that I had even prayed to the Lord and asked Him to reveal Himself to me. But God did not forget. The "ball was in His court" now, and He was doing an internal work in me, setting me up for the next step.

Some weeks later, as I thought about things one evening, God "visited" me and gave me a revelation of Christ. I remembered in a flash that I had asked God to come into my life, and suddenly, in a moment of revelation, I knew that Jesus was real, alive, risen from the dead, and Lord, when only a few minutes before my heart had been filled with doubt. How did this happen? Only God knows; but, God is a Person, and He is well able to make Himself known. I am like the man who was healed of blindness in the ninth chapter of the gospel of John: I don't know how God did it. I just know that I am grateful.

Although my new birth came in 1971, I found I needed to meet God in a fresh new way. I was forced by circumstances over which I had no control to seek the Lord in earnest. God will give us what we need to endure our trial with faith, but we need to seek Him. If we seek Him with all our hearts, the Bible says that we will find Him.

> *Ask and it will be given to you; seek and you will find;*
> *knock and the door will be opened for you.*
> *8 For everyone who asks receives, and the one who seeks finds,*
> *and to the one who knocks, the door will be opened.*
> *Matthew 7:7-8*

Plenty of people in the Bible had to face their fears in order to receive a blessing. As mentioned before, Jacob found God as he faced his greatest fear, meeting his brother Esau, who years earlier had vowed to kill him and who was then coming with an entourage of 400 men to do God knows what! When God requires that we face our greatest fears, it is time to get alone with Him and hang on until He gives us the blessing that is hidden in the trial. Never doubt that it is there.

> *And we know that all things work together for good*
> *for those who love God, who are called according to his purpose,*
> *29 because those whom he foreknew he also predestined to be*
> *conformed to the image of his Son, that his Son would be*
> *the firstborn among many brothers and sisters.*
> *30 And those he predestined, he also called; and those he called,*
> *he also justified; and those he justified, he also glorified.*

31 What then shall we say about these things?
If God is for us, who can be against us?
32 Indeed, he who did not spare his own Son,
but gave him up for us all — how will he not also,
along with him, freely give us all things?
33 Who will bring any charge against God's elect?
It is God who justifies. 34 Who is the one who will condemn?
Christ is the one who died (and more than that, he was raised),
who is at the right hand of God,
and who also is interceding for us.
35 Who will separate us from the love of Christ?
Will trouble, or distress, or persecution, or famine,
or nakedness, or danger, or sword?
36 As it is written, "For your sake we encounter death all day long;
we were considered as sheep to be slaughtered."
37 No, in all these things we have complete victory
through him who loved us!
38 For I am convinced that neither death, nor life,
nor angels, nor heavenly rulers, nor things that are present,
nor things to come, nor powers, 39 nor height, nor depth,
nor anything else in creation will be able to separate us
from the love of God in Christ Jesus our Lord.
Romans 8:28-39

SEEING GOD'S SMILE

*Jacob said, "Please. If you can find it in your heart
to welcome me, accept these gifts.
When I saw your face, it was as the face of God smiling on me.*
Genesis 33:10 (The Message)

KNOWING THAT GOD TRULY LOVES US is a big key to having overcoming faith. Some believers have a feeling that God "loves" them, but fear that He secretly does not like them very much. We have a good reason to think this way since we are so very well acquainted with our own faults and failings. Many of us still think we are on a performance basis in our relationship with God, and we imagine we are quite unworthy of genuine affection from Him. The good news of the gospel, however, is that God loves us to the core, despite our very unlovable traits, and that He is favorably disposed to bless us, all because of what Jesus did for us. When we love someone deeply, it gives us pleasure to show that love through gifts and other favorable acts. That is the way God loves us.

When a severe trial comes, for some it is a confirmation that God's displeasure has been aroused and they are being punished. It is very difficult, if not impossible, to have overcoming faith if we think like that. Perhaps the word "trial" is part of the problem, since it brings to mind a courtroom setting in which we may see ourselves as the accused. If we substitute the word "test" for "trial," we may obtain a better grasp of what God is doing. Tests reveal to us what we know and how far we have come in our training and maturity. They are meant to be passed, but, if we fail one, God does not discard us. Instead we must go back to the Book, the Bible, to study some more and then go back to God, our life coach, for some more internal work. Tests are good, not bad. God is not hurting us by sending tribulation and pressures our way: He is actually helping us. The Apostle Paul wrote:

> *For our momentary, light suffering is producing for us*
> *an eternal weight of glory far beyond all comparison.*
> *2 Corinthians 4:17*

We cannot grow spiritually without encountering tests and tribulation along the way and using them to learn how to overcome by faith. It's analogous to a butterfly struggling to escape its cocoon. If someone tries to "help" the insect by tearing open the cocoon, the butterfly will be robbed of its God-given opportunity to strengthen and develop its wings. It is through the struggle to get out of the cocoon that the butterfly becomes strong enough to fly. As we encounter and struggle with tests and tribulations, our faith and ability to persevere will grow.

> *My brothers and sisters, consider it nothing but joy*
> *when you fall into all sorts of trials,*
> *3 because you know that the testing of your faith*
> *produces endurance. 4 And let endurance have its perfect effect,*
> *so that you will be perfect and complete,*
> *not deficient in anything.*
> *James 1:2-4*

In adversity, we learn that God is faithful and true and we grow strong spiritually. Most of us routinely seek to avoid or quickly escape tribulations. Rather, we should embrace any that God sends our way and seek to profit from them.

Jacob could not escape his meeting with Esau. God had commanded him to return to his homeland, where his brother awaited. Jacob could not discern his brother's attitude toward him all those years after he had deceived their father and taken the blessing; but things didn't look good when it was reported to him that Esau was coming to meet him with four hundred armed men. Jacob feared that he might soon die. When Esau instead welcomed him back, it was for Jacob like an encounter with God Himself.

Think about it: after Jacob wrestled with the angel and subsequently surrendered, whatever followed was sure to be God's will. Can you see the divine logic in this? Surrender to God insures the carrying out of His will. When Esau "buried the hatchet" and hugged him, Jacob saw God's hand in it all. Likewise, as we face our own personal fears, if we surrender the outcome to God, we will ultimately encounter God in and through the trial.

This is part of understanding and submitting to God's sovereignty. God is never the author of evil or sin, but nothing can come into our lives without His permission. Therefore, we can and should acknowledge Him in all things and seek Him in the midst of all things.

> *Trust in the Lord with all your heart,*
> *and do not rely on your own understanding.*
> *6 Acknowledge him in all your ways,*
> *and he will make your paths straight.*
> Proverbs 3:5-6

God has a purpose for everything in our lives. We just need to find it, which happens more easily when we surrender to God's will and purpose. Our purpose is found in His purposes. In fact, it is only in the context of His sovereign will that our lives make sense. What before had been terrifying for Jacob, now became the venue in which he beheld God's smile. When we go through trials and tribulations with an attitude of faith and an expectation of blessing, we will come to know God in a new way and be able to see His smile.

Do we know that God is smiling at us, or do we imagine that His face is clouded, angry, or frowning in displeasure? The priestly blessing from Numbers reveals that God is indeed smiling at us, or, as the literal Hebrew says, "shining" upon us.

> *The LORD bless you and protect you;*
> *25 The LORD make his face to shine upon you,*
> *and be gracious to you;*
> *26 The LORD lift up his countenance upon*
> *you and give you peace.*
> Numbers 6:24-26

A smile is one of the most effective ways to communicate our pleasure in another person. God takes pleasure in His people because we are perfectly pleasing to Him in and through His Son. We are completely justified, accepted, and blessed in Christ.

> *For he chose us in Christ before the foundation of the world*
> *that we may be holy and unblemished in his sight in love.*
> *5 He did this by predestining us to adoption*
> *as his sons through Jesus Christ,*
> *according to the pleasure of his will —*
> *6 to the praise of the glory of his grace*
> *that he has freely bestowed on us in his dearly loved Son.*
> *7 In him we have redemption through his blood,*
> *the forgiveness of our trespasses,*
> *according to the riches of his grace*
> *8 that he lavished on us in all wisdom and insight.*
> *Ephesians 1:4-8*

Yes, God is smiling at us, but do we believe it yet? If you are not convinced, I encourage you to seek the Lord until he shows you the truth about his amazing grace.

A QUICK REVIEW

*Finally, my brothers and sisters,
rejoice in the Lord!
To write this again is no trouble to me,
and it is a safeguard for you.*
Philippians 3:1

SINCE THE REASON I have written this book is to help you survive and thrive in the midst of a severe trial, I believe it is a good idea to review what we have been learning. We often learn best by repetition. Please bear with me if this seems a little tedious, but I believe it will be profitable. Let's list the major points that we have covered so far.

1. Everyone is going to encounter severe trials and tests during his or her lifetime. If you are not in one now, get ready.

2. God is sovereign over all things. Although God is not the author of evil, He does allow suffering to come into our lives to accomplish His own purposes. It is vital that we first acknowledge Him in all things before we start flailing away at the enemy. The devil cannot touch us without God's allowing it, and he can only afflict us within divinely imposed limits.

3. God is loving, wise, and strong. We can safely trust God in every situation. He is never caught off guard nor lacks understanding of what to do. Neither does He lack the ability to make things work out for our good.

4. It is proper to praise God always since the Bible tells us that He is working all things together for our good and His

glory. An attitude of praise works to develop ever increasing faith for our present situation. Faith-based praise is a proper response in every trial.

5. We must hang on to God with all our might until we receive the blessing that is contained in our trial. If we go through a trial without receiving the hidden blessing, we may have wasted our time.

6. If we seek the Lord, He will tell us what we need to know that will enable us to endure and overcome in the trial. A trial is designed to drive us toward the Lord and open the door for a blessing.

7. We need to become convinced that God loves us unconditionally and not view our trial as evidence of His displeasure or rejection. Even if our testing comes as a result of God's discipline in our lives, God's love is unwavering. Grace is always available. God is smiling at His beloved children behind the obscuring clouds of the current test.

If we can put these principles into practice, we will be well on our way to experiencing victory through Christ.

WE ARE NEVER ALONE

*Then I will ask the Father, and he will give you
another Advocate to be with you forever.*
John 14:16

ALL THAT JESUS ACCOMPLISHED through His sacrificial death and glorious resurrection are beyond the scope of this book, but two of the most important things He did was to reconcile us to the Father and give to us the indwelling Holy Spirit. Combining these two wonderful realities with the promises found in God's Word, what more could anyone want or need?

*[We] can pray this because his divine power
has bestowed on us everything necessary for life and godliness
through the rich knowledge of the one
who called us by his own glory and excellence.*
2 Peter 1:3

Do we have any conception of the enormity of this gift of God's indwelling Spirit? He is called the Paraclete, which is Greek for the "One called alongside." He is God at our side, Who helps us, acts as our intercessor, our advocate, our defender, our best friend, and our strength. He is God living inside of us! He is the Person we always wanted to be. He is the grace of God revealed to us and living through us.

When David hid in the wilderness to avoid King Saul's attempts to kill him, men gathered at his side to help him. On one occasion, some men from Benjamin came to his encampment. Here is what the Bible records.

*Other Benjamites and some men from Judah
also came to David in his stronghold.*

*17 David went out to meet them and said to them,
"If you have come to me in peace, to help me,
I am ready to have you unite with me.
But if you have come to betray me
to my enemies when my hands are free from violence,
may the God of our fathers see it and judge you."
18 Then the Spirit came upon Amasai, chief of the Thirty,
and he said: "We are yours, O David!
We are with you, O son of Jesse!
Success, success to you, and success to those who help you,
for your God will help you."
So David received them and made them leaders
of his raiding bands.
1 Chronicles 12:16-18 (NIV)*

In verse 18, the English phrase, "the Spirit came upon Amasai," in Hebrew literally says, "the Spirit clothed Himself with Amasai." This wording is only used three times in the entire Bible, with a powerful meaning each time. The Holy Spirit had something important to say and needed a person to speak through. I believe that Amasai was not merely speaking his own thoughts, although his heart was in full agreement. He was speaking God's heart toward David. I believe we do no injustice to the Scriptures if we make a general application here. What the Spirit spoke to David through Amasai, He speaks to all believers. Through the blessing of the New Covenant, the Holy Spirit has been given to each believer. God's Spirit is "for" us. He has made us more than conquerors.

Let's break down Amasai's statement.

1. The Spirit of God is "ours". He is fully committed to us.

2. God will give us "success", or the Hebrew "shalom", which means peace, prosperity, health, victory and success.

3. God will help us.

This brings us right back to the word "Paraclete." The Holy Spirit's ministry is still the same. He is our fully committed, always-with-us

Helper Who gives us success and peace in any and every situation. We are never alone and never without help.

> *Peace I leave with you; my peace I give to you;*
> *I do not give it to you as the world does.*
> *Do not let your hearts be distressed or lacking in courage.*
> *John 14:27*

Our responsibility is to trust and rely on the One Who is faithfully committed to our success as we pursue God's will.

THE LORD IS MY KEEPER

Your eyes saw me when I was inside the womb.
All the days ordained for me were recorded in your scroll
before one of them came into existence.
Psalm 139:16

THERE IS NOTHING LIKE A BRUSH WITH DEATH to teach us a few important lessons about life. After I received the unwelcome news that my PSA number had suddenly jumped, I found a new ability to focus on God. Imagine that! During the days of deciding what action to take, I continued to pray and read the Bible. The verse from Psalm 139 quoted above became very real and relevant. I saw with fresh insight that the days of my life and the day of my death were completely in God's hands. No cancer would be able to take me out ahead of God's timetable, and I would be foolish to flail about in worry if indeed now was God's appointed time to take me home to be with Him! I was learning first hand that God is my Keeper.

In Old Testament times, a "keeper" was one who watched over another person, guaranteeing his welfare at the expense of his own. King David was Saul's armor bearer and was a most closely trusted protector who stood by the king. Human "keepers" must sleep, however, and cannot be always vigilant; but, God never slumbers or sleeps. He is the consummate Keeper!

My help comes from the LORD,
the Creator of heaven and earth!
3 May he not allow your foot to slip!
May your protector not sleep!
4 Look! Israel's protector does not sleep or slumber!
Psalm 121:2-4

God was our Keeper even before we were ever born, which the theme verse for this chapter makes abundantly clear. The period we spent in the womb was a time when we were completely helpless and in desperate need of a protector. The mother's womb was designed by God to be the ultimate "safe place" where a baby can grow and develop in complete security. This is one reason why abortion is such a travesty and betrayal of God's design for motherhood. God watches over and protects, or keeps, every child in the womb. Even when a pregnancy is terminated, God is there as that child's protector or keeper. God will take them into the eternal safety of heaven should human parents fail in their role as protectors or should some other enemy unleashed by Adam's sin, such as disease, attack the developing child.

But as for us believers, Ephesians 1:3 says that God chose us in Christ before the foundation of the world. This was far before conception ever took place. Being "in Christ" is the ultimate place of protection, a secret haven for all believers. For evil to touch us, it must reach us in our "safe place," which is in Christ Himself.

> *Keep thinking about things above, not things on the earth,*
> *3 for you have died and your life is hidden with Christ in God.*
> *Colossians 3:2-3*

Why then are we anxious when we encounter threatening circumstances? It is because we do not truly know or believe that God is sovereign, committed to be our Keeper, and able to ultimately protect us. The Bible teaches us that God has set a limit to our days here on earth. Jesus has the keys of hell and death; therefore, the devil is not going to sneak up on us and take us out before God's set time.

> *When I saw him I fell down at his feet as though I were dead,*
> *but he placed his right hand on me and said: "Do not be afraid!*
> *I am the first and the last, 18 and the one who lives!*
> *I was dead, but look, now I am alive — forever and ever —*
> *and I hold the keys of death and of Hades!*
> *Revelation 1:17-18*

During His earthly ministry, Jesus was able to pass through hostile crowds without harm because His "time had not yet come." Our safe passage here on earth is also guaranteed by the One Who keeps us during our allotted time of life. Worry is fruitless and dishonors God. It is our unbelief surfacing for all to see.

> *And which of you by worrying can add*
> *even one hour to his life?*
> Matthew 6:27

Worry reveals that we do not believe God is trustworthy. However, if we know that God will keep us no matter what happens, we will have great boldness in times of testing and adversity. God is Master over life and death. We are His and in His hands. And when it is His chosen time for us to leave this earthly life behind, we would be fools to resist. The One who kept us before we were born keeps us now and will forever more.

> *The LORD will protect you from all harm;*
> *he will protect your life.*
> *8 The LORD will protect you in all you do,*
> *now and forevermore.*
> Psalm 121:7-8

Some people, however, have experienced some very difficult and confusing things in life. It seemed as if God did not "keep" them during those times. Why would God allow such suffering? Why didn't He do something about it? Such a person may question whether God can safely be trusted now, since He seemed to be absent back then. As harsh as this may seem, if we think like this, we have fallen for the biggest lie of all – that God is not trustworthy! This is the falsehood Satan used to trick Adam and Eve into eating the forbidden fruit. This is the lie Satan will use whenever he can. It is very effective, and people easily fall for it, especially if we have suffered without understanding why God allowed it to happen. Think of it, though. God has proved his love for us through Christ's death on the cross. All He asks is that we trust Him and live a life that demonstrates that confidence. If we fail to trust God, we fail deeply - a very sobering thought. This is a test we must pass for the sake of God's glory and honor!

If we find it difficult to fully trust God, it is important that we make the decision to believe what the Bible says is true rather than surrender to our own logic and reasoning based on what we have seen, heard or experienced. We are not always capable of accurately judging why God allows certain things to happen. However, the Bible tells us that God uses even the most difficult things in our lives to work good for us. We must believe that truth, no matter what. Our spiritual well-being depends on it.

If instead we choose to believe something that contradicts God's Word, we are guilty of erecting what the Bible calls a "stronghold." This is a logical argument that stands in opposition to truth and gets in between us and a true revelation of God.

> *...for the weapons of our warfare are not human weapons,*
> *but are made powerful by God for tearing down strongholds.*
> *We tear down arguments 5 and every arrogant obstacle*
> *that is raised up against the knowledge of God,*
> *and we take every thought captive to make it obey Christ.*
> *2 Corinthians 10:4-5*

If we have succumbed to such faulty reasoning, we should repent and make the choice to believe the truth. At least we can ask God to help us be free from our lie-based strongholds. A good prayer is to ask the Lord to make us willing to be willing. God is indeed our Keeper and deserves our full confidence. We glorify God by choosing to believe the truth about Him and deciding to trust in Him.

Often the reason we may cling to negative arguments against God's truth is because we have suffered some kind of emotional wound that needs healing. Jesus is the great Healer who will set us free from the deep pain which fuels the lie, if we bring the wound to Him. Many times this is not something we can do very well on our own. We may need help from our brothers and sisters to receive the healing we need. The struggle to believe what the Bible says is true is likely a struggle with hidden, pain-filled, lie-based strongholds. It is paramount that we address these, because our faith is the key to victory, and faith is based on believing God's truth and relying on His character. Coming to the place where we can believe with all our hearts that God loves us and will "keep" us is one of the most important things we will ever do.

TAKING THE STING OUT OF DEATH

Where, O death, is your victory? Where, O death, is your sting?
1 Corinthians 15:55

MANY PEOPLE SUFFER from a deeply seated fear of death that robs them of joy and holds them in bondage. The author of the Letter to the Hebrews gives us the welcome news that Jesus came to solve this problem and liberate those of us who have been held captive.

Therefore, since the children share in flesh and blood,
he likewise shared in their humanity,
so that through death he could destroy the one who holds
the power of death (that is, the devil),
15 and set free those who were held in
slavery all their lives by their fear of death.
Hebrews 2:14-15

Eventually our natural physical life must come to an end. There is a sting to death. It is the end of our earthly dreams and ambitions. It is a temporary separation from those we love. It is a departure from what we know in order to face what is now largely unknown.

The Bible tells us that sin is the sting of death. When a Brown Recluse spider stings a person, the usual result is death to the tissue around the bite. The human race was stung by sin and continues to be stung every day. Death always accompanies this bite. The power of that first sting has ravaged all of creation. Death is unnatural in the sense that it was not a part of God's original design. God Who is Life itself made us to live; therefore, death is a contradiction of Who God is.

Even though all human beings must deal with the aftershocks of sin (which include God's judgment of sin via death), Christ has provided victory through His cross and resurrection. The Law, on the other hand, gives sin and death a strangle hold on the human race by clearly pointing out and condemning us for our sinfulness. In order to set us free, God had to introduce what C.S. Lewis calls a "deeper magic" in his tales of Narnia. The Bible calls it God's hidden wisdom.

> *Now we do speak wisdom among the mature,*
> *but not a wisdom of this age or of the rulers of this age,*
> *who are perishing.*
> *7 Instead we speak the wisdom of God,*
> *hidden in a mystery, that God determined before the ages*
> *for our glory.*
> *8 None of the rulers of this age understood it.*
> *If they had known it,*
> *they would not have crucified the Lord of glory.*
> *1 Corinthians 2:6-8*

Christ came to take our sin upon Himself. He actually became sin and received the attached judgment of death, so that we could become the righteousness of God in Him.

> *God made the one who did not know sin to be sin for us,*
> *so that in him we would become the righteousness of God.*
> *2 Corinthians 5:21*

As a result, we have been blessed in several ways, which include the gift of eternal life. Now, as Jesus proclaimed, even though we die physically, we shall live spiritually. In fact, in reality we shall never die because He is the Resurrection and will someday raise our physical bodies back to life.

> *Jesus said to her,*
> *"I am the resurrection and the life.*
> *The one who believes in me will live even if he dies,*
> *26 and the one who lives and believes in me will never die.*
> *Do you believe this?"*
> *John 11:25-26*

Jesus is now the Lord of Life as well as Lord over death. He has the keys of hell and death. Our lives and physical death are now exclusively under His authority. What then is physical death for the believer? How we view death will greatly influence whether we fear it or not. Death no longer should be viewed as a final separation or end, but as a homecoming and a beginning. The Bible tells us that God regards the death of His saints as a precious thing. (Psalm 116:15) The Hebrew word here means "precious, splendid, rare or weighty." For God, death is His opportunity to welcome us into a new realm and dimension of life in which we can more fully enjoy Him, and He enjoy us. Look what Paul wrote.

> *Therefore we are always full of courage,*
> *and we know that as long as we are alive here on earth*
> *we are absent from the Lord —*
> *7 for we live by faith, not by sight.*
> *8 Thus we are full of courage and would prefer*
> *to be away from the body and at home with the Lord.*
> *9 So then whether we are alive or away,*
> *we make it our ambition to please him.*
> *2 Corinthians 5:6-9*

Paul actually looked forward to his own demise because he had already been given a glimpse of what awaited him in the heavenly realms. If we could see as clearly as Paul did, we would never fear death. May God open our eyes to the true nature of our physical death! It is the doorway to life eternal in the very presence of God. Jesus could not wait to get back to His Father. We really have little idea yet of how good our homecoming will be!

> *But just as it is written,*
> *"Things that no eye has seen, or ear heard, or mind imagined,*
> *are the things God has prepared for those who love him."*
> *1 Corinthians 2:9*

If you are facing death, now is the time to meditate on the victory over death we have in Christ. Now is the time to participate in the peace that passes understanding. We must learn to hear the voice of the Good Shepherd calling out to us:

> *Jesus said to her,*
> *"I am the resurrection and the life.*
> *The one who believes in me will live even if he dies,*
> *26 and the one who lives and believes in me will never die.*
> *Do you believe this?"*
> *John 11:25-26*

Do we believe this? The things we are facing or will face eventually are designed to provide a setting for the Spirit of God to reveal to us in a personal way that Jesus is our Life, a life that never ends and is absolutely fulfilling – eternal, resurrection life.

> *So Jesus said to them again,*
> *"I tell you the solemn truth, I am the door for the sheep.*
> *8 All who came before me were thieves and robbers,*
> *but the sheep did not listen to them.*
> *9 I am the door. If anyone enters through me, he will be saved,*
> *and will come in and go out, and find pasture.*
> *10 The thief comes only to steal and kill and destroy;*
> *I have come so that they may have life,*
> *and may have it abundantly.*
> *John 10:7-10*

A confrontation with death, then, is actually an invitation from God to know the Lord Jesus Christ as the Resurrection and the Life. The light shines most brightly in the worst darkness.

REJECTING REJECTION

*And we have come to know and to believe
the love that God has in us.
God is love, and the one who resides in love resides in God,
and God resides in him. 17 By this love is perfected with us,
so that we may have confidence in the day of judgment,
because just as Jesus is, so also are we in this world.
18 There is no fear in love, but perfect love drives out fear,
because fear has to do with punishment.
The one who fears punishment has not been perfected in love.
19 We love because he loved us first.
1 John 4:16-19*

ONE OF THE MAIN REASONS some people are afraid of dying is because they fear God will ultimately reject them at the judgment seat. We know from the Bible that we will be judged according to our works, and most level headed people realize that their works simply don't add up to enough "points" to satisfy God's perfect righteousness. Therefore we instinctively expect to encounter God's displeasure when our lives are examined by Him in righteous judgment. We fear rejection.

Rejection took root in the human race the day Adam and Eve sinned. They hid in the garden because they were afraid that God would reject their nakedness. They were ashamed. Shame is a sign of rejection working in our lives. Adam and Eve had good reason to be ashamed, too. In a rebellious attempt to be like God, they had violated the one prohibition God had given them. They had rejected the Creator and now were experiencing the flip side of that rejection - their own.

Interestingly, though, God did not, in fact, reject them. Instead, He disciplined them severely with a curse and expulsion from the garden; but along with that He gave them the promise of a Savior and clothed them with animal skins, an act of great mercy that foreshadowed the coming covering of righteousness that Jesus would provide through His death and resurrection. Adam and Eve stood before God's judgment seat without any hope for mercy, but received it nevertheless. How much more should we who have received the reconciliation provided by Christ expect to receive mercy when we stand before that same God one day!

> *Much more then, because we have now been declared righteous*
> *by his blood, we will be saved through him from God's wrath.*
> *10 For if while we were enemies we were*
> *reconciled to God through the death of his Son,*
> *how much more, since we have been reconciled,*
> *will we be saved by his life?*
> *11 Not only this, but we also rejoice in God*
> *through our Lord Jesus Christ,*
> *through whom we have now received this reconciliation.*
> *Romans 5:9-11*

When I first faced the possibility of having prostate cancer, some two years before the confirmed diagnosis, I felt fear come into my heart one evening. Up until that time, although I was a little "on edge," I had not had to deal with real fear. As someone familiar with lie-based strongholds, I realized immediately that my fear revealed that I believed a lie somewhere in my heart. Intellectually and theologically I knew that death is nothing to be feared for believers in Christ, but the heart has its own reasons for believing what it does. I needed the Lord, the Wonderful Counselor, to expose the root of this lie and replace it with liberating truth.

In prayer, I asked the Lord to reveal to me what was going on. Immediately I heard the Lord speak in my heart, "You don't think that I really want you." I knew that this was the truth. Intellectually I understood that I was accepted in Christ, but on a "gut level" I doubted it. I believed one thing logically but something altogether different in my heart. Our emotions feed off of what we believe in our hearts; hence, the fear. My heart was where the lie behind the fear resided.

And since faith resides in the heart, too, fear was trumping faith as a result of my believing a lie instead of believing the truth.

As quickly as I heard God speak those words to me, I began to think of various verses from Scripture that refuted the lie that God did not really want me. The first thing I thought was that I should not doubt that God wanted me since Christ died for me. (How basic is that? But I still needed to "hear it" again in my heart, this time from God Himself!) God once for all time proved His love and acceptance of me on the cross. Why would He now reject the one for whom He had paid such a dear price? It wasn't as if He did not know beforehand what I would be like. He knew, but chose me any way. Praise the Lord!

This is one of the great lessons we learn from Scripture. God chooses the unlovely and unlikely, simply because it gives Him pleasure to do so. Jacob is a perfect example. Could there have been a more unlikely choice than he? He was a deceiver and conniver. Jacob's trust in God often waivered; nevertheless, God chose him to be a father in the faith! Resolve in your hearts that God's choice of you to be His child did not and does not, nor ever will, depend on your performance. When God chooses to love a person, nothing on earth, in heaven, or in hell can alter that.

> *No, in all these things we have complete victory*
> *through him who loved us!*
> *38 For I am convinced that neither death,*
> *nor life, nor angels, nor heavenly rulers,*
> *nor things that are present, nor things to come, nor powers,*
> *39 nor height, nor depth, nor anything else in creation*
> *will be able to separate us from the love of God*
> *in Christ Jesus our Lord.*
> *Romans 8:37-39*

Next I began to meditate on the passage of Scripture that opens this chapter. I realized that my fear was based on a lack of confidence in God's love for me. God began to wash over my soul with a fresh new revelation of His love that pushed the fear right out. Faith in God's love is the most powerful weapon against fear that we have.

> *If anyone confesses that Jesus is the Son of God,*
> *God resides in him and he in God.*
> *16 And we have come to know and to believe*
> *the love that God has in us.*
> *God is love, and the one who resides in love resides in God,*
> *and God resides in him.*
> *17 By this love is perfected with us,*
> *so that we may have confidence in the day of judgment,*
> *because just as Jesus is, so also are we in this world.*
> *18 There is no fear in love, but perfect love drives out fear,*
> *because fear has to do with punishment.*
> *The one who fears punishment has not been perfected in love.*
> *19 We love because he loved us first.*
> *1 John 4:15-19*

To the degree that we fear being rejected by God, we have failed to understand and receive His love that comes to us in Christ. Yes, we will be judged after we die, and, on the positive side, we will be rewarded for the works of faith done during our lives; but our acceptance into God's family is not based on our works at all, but on Christ's. The only work we must do to pass from death to life and to escape eternal condemnation and rejection is to believe on the Son and on what He did to save us.

> *So then they said to him,*
> *"What must we do to accomplish the deeds God requires?"*
> *29 Jesus replied, "This is the deed God requires —*
> *to believe in the one whom he sent."*
> *John 6:28-29*

Life is an opportunity for us to grow in the knowledge and revelation of God's love for us. God's love is the most freeing power in the universe. Once we are perfected in love, we will serve God from the right motives - not to obtain His acceptance, but because we love Him in return. It is time for us to rise up and reject rejection and receive in its place the amazing love of God.

> *I tell you the solemn truth,*
> *the one who hears my message and believes the one who sent me*
> *has eternal life and will not be condemned,*
> *but has crossed over from death to life.*
> *John 5:24*

SURRENDER, UNCONDITIONAL PEACE AND THE SECRET PLACE

Rejoice in the Lord always.
Again I say, rejoice!
5 Let everyone see your gentleness. The Lord is near!
6 Do not be anxious about anything.
Instead, in every situation, through prayer and petition
with thanksgiving, tell your requests to God.
7 And the peace of God that surpasses all understanding
will guard your hearts and minds in Christ Jesus.
Philippians 4:4-7

IN WARFARE, peace often comes through one side unconditionally surrendering. As long as two opposing wills still contend, there can be no peace. In a severe trial, divine peace comes through our unconditional surrender to God. Our wills must submit to His. We are surrounded by Satan's demonic forces who wish to destroy us, but, oddly enough, sometimes we are our own worst enemies. Our sin and the fear and mistrust in our hearts toward God sabotage our efforts to be true to Him. God has a plan for our lives, but if we stubbornly and fearfully refuse to go along with that plan, we can end up in an unprotected place outside of God's best for our lives, in need of His correction and deliverance.

Surrender to God and His will requires that we lay down our own agendas and our desire to control our lives and "accept" whatever God allows to come into our lives. It means that we must be open to the possibility that God will require us to go through something we dread. Unless we unconditionally surrender to God, we cannot have unconditional peace.

By "accepting" I do not mean that we passively submit to evil. Instead, when we find ourselves under attack, our first responsibility is to acknowledge that God is sovereign. Unless He allows something to enter our lives, it will not happen. We are not hereby declaring that God is the author of evil, sin, suffering, or sickness. We are saying that God's sovereignty transcends all these things in a magnificent and mysterious way that is beyond explaining. Accepting what God allows to come into our lives means that we acknowledge His sovereignty in every situation, seek Him and His will first, and then engage the enemy as directed.

When the Philistines attacked David, his first response was to seek the Lord Who gave him specific instructions regarding how to proceed. Too often Christians flail about in sometimes misguided attempts to fend off the attack rather than seek the Lord Who may be allowing the attack in order to do a deep work in the believer. When Jesus stood before Pilate, our Lord declared that the Roman ruler could only do to Him what God allowed.

> *So Pilate said, "Do you refuse to speak to me?*
> *Don't you know I have the authority to release you,*
> *and to crucify you?"*
> *11 Jesus replied, "You would have no authority over me at all,*
> *unless it was given to you from above.*
> *Therefore the one who handed me over*
> *to you is guilty of greater sin."*
> *John 19:10-11*

Before going to the cross, at which time darkness would temporarily rule, Jesus first did business with His heavenly Father - the real Ruler in every situation. When we are about to enter a trial or are in the middle of one, we should first go to God and be sure our hearts and wills are submitted to what He wants to accomplish in our lives through the trial. It is only against that backdrop of trust and submission that we can know more perfectly what other actions we must take. If instead we simply begin to engage in what we might want to call "spiritual warfare," we may find ourselves unhappily resisting God Himself. Imagine if Jesus had rebuked Satan instead of surrendering to death as God's Lamb! This is what Peter advised his Master to do, but Jesus rebuked his misguided friend by telling him that he did not have the things of

God in mind. Imagine how foolish it would be for us to fearfully rebuke a pending trial that may be the avenue to our knowing Christ as Provider, Healer, or in whatever other way we need to know Him! Check in with God first. Find out what He wants to do; then, join His program. This is what it means to have Christ as Lord.

A severe trial will often cause whatever rebelliousness and fear we still may have deeply buried in our hearts to bubble to the surface. God knew it was there all along, but we may be surprised to discover what is hidden inside of us. The fire of affliction tests and reveals our hidden motives and the nature and strength of our faith. If we know God loves us enough to expose these things in order to deliver us, we will better be able to endure the process by faith.

Unless we go through the fire, we never know for sure what is inside us. Until we face our fears, our faith is somewhat of a mystery. Soldiers who have never been in combat wonder what they will do under fire. No one can know for sure ahead of time. Once we go through our first battle, however, we know. That which we dread can become for us the gateway into great faith and confidence after we have faced it and found that God's grace enables us to overcome.

Job had to endure what he feared so that his subtle self-righteousness and proud indignation against God would bubble to the surface. God was far more interested in revealing Himself in a greater way to Job than in keeping him pain free. When we realize that character transformation is a higher priority than our comfort and ease, we will begin to better understand God's ways. If we embrace God's ways, we will be pliable in His hands for Him to mold us how He wishes.

As long as our peace hinges on a certain set of conditions or a certain answer to prayer, we will always be subject to our circumstances and miss out on experiencing real and lasting peace. Being enslaved to our circumstances is a terrible way to live because we can never be completely at rest. What we dread could be just around the corner... and then what? It is no use trying to insulate ourselves from what we fear by "having enough faith." Faith was never designed to protect us from trials: rather, faith keeps us while we are in trials. Ponder Christ's words:

> *I have told you these things so that in me you may have peace.*
> *In the world you have trouble and suffering,*
> *but take courage —*
> *I have conquered the world.*
> *John 16:33*

If we believe that trusting in Christ is our ticket to a trouble free life, we are in for a shock. Nothing could be further from the truth. We are actually appointed to tribulations.

> *We sent Timothy, our brother and fellow worker for God*
> *in the gospel of Christ, to strengthen you*
> *and encourage you about your faith,*
> *3 so that no one would be shaken by these afflictions.*
> *For you yourselves know that we are destined for this.*
> *1 Thessalonians 3:2-3*

Trials, afflictions, suffering and tribulations work for us. They teach us perseverance and build character. Here is what Paul wrote to the church in Rome.

> *Not only this, but we also rejoice in sufferings,*
> *knowing that suffering produces endurance,*
> *4 and endurance, character, and character, hope.*
> *5 And hope does not disappoint,*
> *because the love of God has been poured out in our hearts*
> *through the Holy Spirit who was given to us.*
> *Romans 5:3-5*

It is only when we reconcile ourselves to the fact that life will contain many difficult trials, and only when we choose to surrender to God in the midst of them, trusting in His love and power to accomplish in us His desire through them, that we are able to have peace that passes understanding. I call this "unconditional peace" because it does not depend on any outward circumstance or condition. Whether we live or die, we have peace. Whether we get the answer we want or not, we have peace. Peace resides in a Person, and His name is Jesus. As we fully surrender to that Person, we receive all of what that Person has and is. One of His titles is the Prince of Peace. His peace becomes our peace, a peace that can never be shaken.

> *Peace I leave with you; my peace I give to you;*
> *I do not give it to you as the world does.*
> *Do not let your hearts be distressed or lacking in courage.*
> *John 14:27*

Moses wrote about this place of surrender and peace. It is a secret place hidden from life's storms and the threats of the enemy. It is a place where God's peace and presence reign undisturbed. We have access to that secret place by surrendering unconditionally to God's will for our lives.

> *As for you, the one who lives in the shelter*
> *of the sovereign One, and resides in the*
> *protective shadow of the mighty king —*
> *2 I say this about the LORD,*
> *my shelter and my stronghold,*
> *my God in whom I trust.*
> *Psalm 91:1-2*

Surrendering to God's will and plan for our lives will not make us passive. In fact, we will find that, as we unconditionally surrender to God, great faith will rise up in our hearts - faith to overcome.

UNCONDITIONAL PRAISE - THE GATEWAY TO OVERCOMING FAITH

Always rejoice,
17 constantly pray,
18 in everything give thanks.
For this is God's will for you in Christ Jesus.
1 Thessalonians 5:16-18

THE ROAD TO THE SECRET PLACE in God's presence, where we are safe from strife and the storms of life, is paved with praise. Unconditional praise means we praise God in every situation, no matter what. This is a corollary of unconditional surrender to the sovereign will of God.

Here is how this works: if God is truly in control of all things and He is working all things together for good in my life, then I can and should praise Him in every situation and circumstance. This is pretty simple logic that is in total harmony with our theme verse for today. When we praise and worship God during a severe trial, it is an expression of our faith in the goodness and keeping power of God. We glorify the Lord through offering such praise because we demonstrate a faith that does not depend on outward circumstances. Such praise is a powerful form of spiritual warfare and will ultimately put us in a place where we can more easily hear God's voice, understand His will, and believe His promises.

May they praise God while they hold a two-edged sword
in their hand, 7 in order to take revenge on the nations,
and punish foreigners. 8 They bind their kings in chains,

> *and their nobles in iron shackles, 9 and execute the judgment*
> *to which their enemies have been sentenced.*
> *All his loyal followers will be vindicated. Praise the LORD!*
> *Psalm 149:6-9*

When we unconditionally surrender to the sovereign will of God in any and every circumstance, understanding that He has a divine purpose in everything and is working things out for our good and His glory, and when we offer to Him unconditional praise in all things, we choose to separate ourselves from anything revolving around our own agenda. We relinquish control, so to speak. Once we do this, there is no hindrance to our hearing God speak to us what is on His heart and what He wants to do in and through our situation. Once we apprehend what God's specific will is, we can then praise Him for what He is going to do. This becomes a prophetic faith proclamation in the form of praise. This releases dynamic, aggressive, overcoming faith that is built upon the foundation of unconditional, surrendered praise.

Unconditional praisers are able to aggressively believe that God will act in their situation without having to wonder if this is just something they dreamed up in a vain attempt to save themselves from pain or testing. Once we have the assurance that we understand God's will and have prayed and believed accordingly, we know we will obtain what we have asked for. This is clearly stated in Scripture. Faith is agreeing with God's will.

> *And this is the confidence that we have before him:*
> *that whenever we ask anything according to his will,*
> *he hears us. 15 And if we know that he hears us*
> *in regard to whatever we ask,*
> *then we know that we have the requests*
> *that we have asked from him.*
> *1 John 5:14-15*

Once again we see that Christianity is paradoxical. How could surrender produce aggressive overcoming faith? It works in the same way that death produces life and serving leads to honor. It is reverse thinking from how the world goes at things, but it works and it is real. You should give it a try. If you journey down the road of unconditional praise, you will arrive at the revelation that Christ is your banner of victory.

> *Indeed, my plans are not like your plans,*
> *and my deeds are not like your deeds,*
> *9 for just as the sky is higher than the earth,*
> *so my deeds are superior to your deeds*
> *and my plans superior to your plans.*
> *Isaiah 55:8-9*

GRACE IS FOR THE "WHATS", NOT THE "WHAT IFS"

*Without being weak in faith,
he considered his own body as dead (because he was about one
hundred years old) and the deadness of Sarah's womb.
20 He did not waver in unbelief about the promise of God
but was strengthened in faith, giving glory to God.
21 He was fully convinced that what God promised
he was also able to do.
Romans 4:19-21*

THE ROAD TO THE SECRET PLACE of God's peace and protection has a few road signs and rules. One is that we cannot afford to go off on any detours of conjecture or into any hypothetical situations unless our faith is up to the task. Real faith is able to look at the problem or challenge we face, at the enemy who threatens us, or at the severe trial we suffer and still have confidence in God. However, God did not design grace to handle wild and uncontrolled rambles into fearful conjectures and "what ifs." When we are in the midst of a severe trial, we must practice self-control in the realm of our thinking. There are certain places we simply cannot go if we wish to keep our faith fires fanned.

When I returned to see my urologist to get the results of the CT scan and bone scan, I was feeling nervous. This was a "moment of truth" that would somewhat define the nature of my looming battle. Was the cancer confined to the prostate, or had it escaped and penetrated my body's defenses? Was the solution for this cancer relatively simple, or was I going to need a big time miracle and/or extensive chemotherapy and radiation? I had to "live for the moment" rather than contemplate "what if" the doctor told me the cancer had spread. We have to be firm with our thoughts, cutting off our fearful conjectures whenever they try to surface. If the answer was what I hoped, then all my worrying would have been for nothing. If the cancer had spread, God would give me the grace to face that, too. In the meantime, I had to concentrate on trusting God - regardless. I had to keep my mind fixed on Him, His love, His faithfulness, His power, and wisdom.

I also had the advantage of God's having spoken a "word" to me from the Psalms. I held to the promise that this would not end in death. When we have a promise from God, it makes it that much easier to limit what we think about. Simply refuse to go outside the boundaries of the promise. If we don't have such a promise, we can make the decision to keep our thoughts within the bounds of His loving promise to keep us in all situations. We might try reading and meditating upon Psalm 23.

The stronger our faith grows, we will be less threatened by our circumstances. Like Abraham, we will be able to look the problem in the eye and still believe. If you are not there yet, simply make the choice to refuse to go anywhere in your thinking where your faith cannot yet handle it. God's grace is sufficient one day and one step at a time.

So then, do not worry about tomorrow,
for tomorrow will worry about itself.
Today has enough trouble of its own.
Matthew 6:34

We must make it our aim to maintain a life of praise, taking our fears and concerns to God in prayer. His promise is to give us His peace.

Rejoice in the Lord always.
Again I say, rejoice!
5 Let everyone see your gentleness. The Lord is near!
6 Do not be anxious about anything. Instead, in every situation,
through prayer and petition with thanksgiving,
tell your requests to God.
7 And the peace of God that surpasses all
understanding will guard your hearts and minds
in Christ Jesus.

*8 Finally, brothers and sisters, whatever is true,
whatever is worthy of respect, whatever is just, whatever is pure,
whatever is lovely, whatever is commendable,
if something is excellent or praiseworthy,
think about these things.
9 And what you learned and received and heard and saw in me,
do these things.
And the God of peace will be with you.
Philippians 4:4-9*

THE ONLY SAFE PLACE IS THE SECRET PLACE

He will surely give me shelter in the day of danger;
he will hide me in his home;
he will place me on an inaccessible rocky summit.
6 Now I will triumph over my enemies who
surround me! I will offer sacrifices in his dwelling place
and shout for joy! I will sing praises to the LORD!
Psalm 27:5-6

IN THE DAYS BEFORE I went through surgery to remove the cancer, I spent time singing an old song from the 1970's during the height of the "Jesus Movement" and the "Charismatic Renewal." Here is how it goes.

> Keep me, Jesus, as the apple of Thine eye.
> Hide me under the shadow of Thy wings.
> Thou, O Lord, must keep me lest I die.
> Keep me, Jesus, as the apple of Thine eye.

It is a simple chorus, but it ministered to my soul. Here is the portion of Scripture from which it was derived.

Accomplish awesome, faithful deeds,
you who powerfully deliver those who look to you
for protection from their enemies.
8 Protect me as you would protect the pupil of your eye!
Hide me in the shadow of your wings!
Psalm 17:7-8

The "apple" of the eye is the pupil. Everyone guards his eyes. It is a basic instinct. We are as precious to God, or even more so, than our eyes are to us. The Lord diligently watches over His people to keep them during both good times and bad. When it seems to us that God has taken a vacation from being our Shepherd, He is still right by our side. In fact, He lives inside us, never to leave. According to our theme verse, it is in the day of trouble that we find special protection in God's secret place. In that place we find covering, secrecy and protection, but not as a cowering rat in a hole. Instead God lifts us up upon a Rock, Christ, and gives us victory over our enemies, filling our mouths with praise.

The secret place is a place of invulnerability, a place of victory, a place of rest. It is God Himself. He is our strong tower and refuge. For the Christian, the secret of life and peace is the knowledge of who we are in Christ and Who He is to and in us. In Christ, the victory is already won. In Christ, we have peace that passes understanding. In Christ, there is unwavering faith. In Christ, is authority and power. He is our secret place.

> *Therefore, if you have been raised with Christ,*
> *keep seeking the things above,*
> *where Christ is, seated at the right hand of God.*
> *2 Keep thinking about things above, not things on the earth,*
> *3 for you have died and your life is hidden with Christ in God.*
> *Colossians 3:1-3*

The secret place is not a place to which we run only when things are rough. The fact is that the only safe place in this universe is God's secret place in Christ. At other times, we may seem to enjoy an external form of safety and security, but it is only a short-lived thing, because this physical life and natural world are passing away. Danger lurks everywhere in our sin-plagued world. Evil people surround us. Demonic hordes seek our downfall and destruction. Satanic strategies are being hatched against us continually. This earth in which we live is not a nice or safe place.

Paul wrote that the entire creation groans as it waits for Christ to come again to set things right. The more we seek to follow God and be an instrument in His hand to rescue the lost and bring deliverance to the hurting, the greater the resistance from the enemy we will experience. What then are we to do? It is simple: run to the secret place of God's presence every day. The enemy cannot get to us there. How do we get there? We just walk right in. In Christ, we have bold and confident access into God's throne room. We can say, "Hello, Father! Can I sit in your lap for a while and enjoy Your love and presence?" The answer is always, "Yes!" Things may be swirling on the outside, but it is always calm in the secret place of God's presence.

*Therefore let us confidently approach the throne of grace
to receive mercy and find grace whenever we need help.
Hebrews 4:16*

REASSESSING PRIORITIES AND PAYING VOWS

Do I eat the flesh of bulls?
Do I drink the blood of goats?
14 Present to God a thank-offering!
Repay your vows to the sovereign One!
15 Pray to me when you are in trouble!
I will deliver you, and you will honor me!"
Psalm 50:13-15

King David prayed:

O LORD, help me understand my mortality
and the brevity of life!
Let me realize how quickly my life will pass!
Psalm 39:4

IT IS A GOOD THING for us to be reminded that our time here on earth in these fleshly bodies is limited so that we can apply ourselves to living as wisely as God would have us live. Moses wrote in another place:

So teach us to consider our mortality,
so that we might live wisely.
Psalm 90:12

When we are in the midst of a severe trial, perhaps one that affects our health or job security or family, we have a wonderful chance to reassess our priorities and make some decisions about how we will live the remainder of our lives. It might be appropriate to "make a vow" to the

Lord that we will dedicate the rest of our days to Him and to service in His Kingdom. Making this "vow" is always the right thing to do if we claim that Jesus is our Lord, but never more so than when God forces us to reconsider our commitment to Him through the pressures of tribulation.

I am not suggesting that we make a "deal" with God – exchanging a pledge of service for His delivering us. Rather, I am suggesting that when we are in dire circumstances we have a golden opportunity to realign our lives according to God's priorities. When things are easy, we tend to to drift. When things are difficult, it is time to reassess. Is this not the history of Israel? It is human nature. That is why we should look at every trial as an opportunity for growth in devotion, faith, obedience, and our knowledge of God. James wrote eloquently about this:

> *My brothers and sisters, consider it nothing but joy*
> *when you fall into all sorts of trials,*
> *3 because you know that the testing of your faith*
> *produces endurance. 4 And let endurance have its perfect effect,*
> *so that you will be perfect and complete,*
> *not deficient in anything.*
> *James 1:2-4*

Christ is Lord of all things, including the details of the lives of His servants. All too often we choose to live according to our own set of values and priorities instead of God's. Sometimes we think that we have "plenty of time" to get around to living more fully for God, but in the midst of a trial perhaps we see that our time will be over before we know it. There is no time like "now" to begin living the way God wants us to live.

There is something God wants from each of us - our hearts, our souls. He is after US and will not be satisfied until we fully surrender to His will.

> *For what benefit is it for a person*
> *to gain the whole world, yet forfeit his life?*
> *37 What can a person give in exchange for his life?*

38 For if anyone is ashamed of me and my words
in this adulterous and sinful generation,
the Son of Man will also be ashamed of him
when he comes in the glory of his Father with the holy angels.
Mark 8:36-38

God desires our praise and willing obedience. He wants our trust. He wants us to live fully, unashamedly, and boldly for Him and His kingdom. There is no need to wait until we are in a "tough place" to finally give God what He desires, but, if we are already there, why not ride the momentum of our trial and pull our lives more fully in line with God's purposes? Why not do it today? Below is a sample prayer you may wish to pray.

Lord, please forgive me for living for my own desires and pleasures. Help me to live the way you want from this day forward. I surrender my life, my health, my wealth, my family, and my future to you. Give me grace to obey you every day. Amen.

GOD'S GYM

*Therefore, since we have been declared righteous by faith,
we have peace with God through our Lord Jesus Christ,
2 through whom we have also obtained access by faith
into this grace in which we stand,
and we rejoice in the hope of God's glory.
3 Not only this, but we also rejoice in sufferings,
knowing that suffering produces endurance,
4 and endurance, character, and character, hope.
5 And hope does not disappoint,
because the love of God has been poured out in our hearts
through the Holy Spirit who was given to us.
Romans 5:1-5*

GYM RATS HAVE A SAYING: "No pain, no gain." Muscles grow strong by being tested, pushed, and stretched beyond what is comfortable. We have heard it said that if we want to grow as a person, we must be willing to get out of our "comfort zone" and try new things, confront our fears and insecurities, and find out "what we are made of." Very few people can oversee their own training adequately. We are usually too soft on ourselves. A good trainer knows how far to push a person before it might lead to injury. A good trainer understands the real limits of his client, not just the imagined ones.

God is the best trainer of all. The Bible says that He will never allow us to be tested beyond our (His) ability (in us) to endure. No, that was not a typo. Notice that I did not say "beyond our ability to endure" all by ourselves. God is not afraid to push us beyond our own human endurance, knowing that it gives us an opportunity to experience His ability in us, which is grace. If He did not do this, how would we ever experience the wonders of grace?

> *For we do not want you to be unaware,*
> *brothers and sisters, regarding the affliction that happened to us in the*
> *province of Asia, that we were burdened excessively,*
> *beyond our strength, so that we despaired even of living.*
> *9 Indeed we felt as if the sentence of death had been passed against*
> *us, so that we would not trust in ourselves*
> *but in God who raises the dead.*
> *2 Corinthians 1:8-9*

As Christians, we often fail in the area of discipline and growth. We are called to embrace the cross and its death sentence to our self-centeredness, but we try to use rubber nails and make sure we have an escape option. The real cross has iron nails and no way out. When we are confronted by something in life that takes us far outside of our comfort zone and from which there is no escape, we have entered God's gym, we have encountered an expression of the cross of Christ. God is our Spiritual Trainer, and He is relentless in the pursuit of our becoming like His Son in character, faith, and obedience. And He is always with us to teach us that his grace is greater than anything He may allow us to face.

Faith is like a muscle. The more we use it, the stronger it grows. In fact, real faith will grow stronger the more it is taxed. Real faith has its genesis and support in God and never fails. Our human version of faith may reach its limit and peter out, but whatever God has put inside us will not. When we come to what we think is the "end of our rope," we will find out how much real faith we have, because true faith is immovable. People who have gone beyond their own ability to endure are often greatly surprised and relieved to discover that God's presence and power inside of them (grace) is more than adequate. When they thought they had run out of steam, they found a peace that passes understanding. It is beyond explanation.

For those of us whose "faith" fails, we should not lose heart. God shows us the limits of our own strength to entice us to seek His all-sufficient grace. God disillusions us when we place our hope in things that cannot succeed and offers Himself in their place. God is the Great Encourager. If you turn to Him, you will find Him. That is His promise.

It is important that we be among those who are regulars at God's gym. Most people are lazy and undisciplined and never choose to do what is necessary to be in good shape. God is working inside us to make us spiritually toned and able to fight. Don't run from His gym. Get a lifetime membership. If you are the kind of person who finds it difficult to maintain personal habits of self-discipline, why not find an accountability partner who will make the journey with you? The more, the merrier!

EVERYTHING IS AGAINST ME!?

*When they were emptying their sacks,
there was each man's bag of money in his sack!
When they and their father saw the bags of money,
they were afraid. 36 Their father Jacob said to them,
"You are making me childless! Joseph is gone. Simeon is gone.
And now you want to take Benjamin!
Everything is against me."
Genesis 42:35-36*

IF WE NEED ENCOURAGEMENT because we feel that we are slow learners in God's graduate courses at Holy Spirit University, we can take heart from the life of Jacob. He is regarded as one of the patriarchs, a father in the faith; yet, in his old age he was still deficient in his ability to fully trust God. In the verse above, he was on the verge of the greatest blessing of his life – a reunion with his son Joseph, but he could not see it with the eyes of faith. He was still interpreting life through the appearance of circumstances instead of trusting in God's loving sovereignty.

Certainly, it looked as if everything was going against old Jacob. He had suffered the loss of his dearest son Joseph years before. He had lost his beloved Rachel. He was living in the midst of a severe famine, and something very weird was happening in Egypt. There was simply no rational explanation. He was being pressured into surrendering Benjamin, his youngest and last remaining child born to Rachel, to the dangers of international travel to a dangerous land at the demand of a nosy, imperious Egyptian official.

God required him to take another big step of faith: he had to let Benjamin go. The words of our mouth will usually reveal the true level of our faith in times like these. When the pressure is on, we revert to what we believe deep down in our hearts, regardless of how polished a theology we may have. Jacob's heart interpreted the events swirling around him as evidence of everything being against him. His fears were getting the best of him; but, what was the reality?

Actually Joseph was orchestrating the events in Egypt, working things out for a glorious reunion with his family. Jacob was about to learn that his beloved son was not only still alive, but ruling in that foreign land as God's provision for him and his family during the famine. What looked so ominous was actually a carefully arranged plan to bless Jacob and his family. Jacob completely misread the events in which he was immersed and spoke words of unbelief; but, the good news is that God's plan for blessing him (and us) did not depend on Jacob or his confession. It depended on Joseph, who was a type or shadow of our Lord Jesus. I hope you see how this applies to your situation. While our faith and confession are indeed important, ultimately our deliverance depends on Jesus.

When events in our lives are apparently out of control and "against us," we must remind ourselves that our Joseph (Jesus) is alive and in control. Our Lord is on the throne and working all things out for our good and His glory. Let's learn from Jacob's failure and determine in our hearts that we will always say: "Everything is for me because God is for me!"

What then shall we say about these things?
If God is for us, who can be against us?
Romans 8:31

THE GOLD STANDARD

*Trust in the LORD with all your heart,
and do not rely on your own understanding.
6 Acknowledge him in all your ways,
and he will make your paths straight.
Proverbs 3:5-6*

THE JOURNEY TO THE SECRET PLACE of God's presence requires that we make some key route decisions along the way. Sooner or later we will come to a fork in the road. Which path we take will make all the difference. We will have to decide whether we will trust God completely with our lives regardless of circumstances and fears, or if we will try to retain personal control based on our own understanding of things.

The "gold standard" is a phrase that is used to describe the very best measurement we have of true value or worth. When it comes to faith, we must choose what will be our own "gold standard": will it be our own understanding of matters or what God's Word says? Proverbs 3:5-6 is a "Core Scripture" for every disciple of Christ. If we don't get this one down, we are not going far in our "walk" with God. Life is a journey, a walk, so to speak, with God. When two people walk together, they need to agree on their destination. When disagreement arises, paths will part. We want to make sure we stay in harmony with God in our walk with Him.

This is no small matter. If we believe that God is really "directing our paths," it will be necessary for us to acknowledge Him in "all our ways" and trust that He is ultimately working out all things for good in our lives. If we do not believe that God is ultimately in control or can be safely trusted to direct our paths, we will see ourselves as being "on our own," trying to figure out the best course of action. If things take a turn for the worse, we will be tempted to panic, wondering if we made the right decision, or asking ourselves if there is even a good decision to be made at all. Perhaps our faith was not strong enough, or maybe we did not pray enough, or perhaps we did not accurately discern God's will. Maybe we disobeyed God and are simply reaping the results. Maybe the devil has gotten the upper hand in our case. The "maybes" will never end unless we settle it in our hearts that God alone will be the gold standard for evaluating every situation and decision. Yes, it is crucial to have faith in God, to obey Him, to hear what He is telling us, and to do spiritual warfare; but, we have to decide whether or not we believe our lives and future ultimately rest with God or are in our own hands.

Solomon declared that everyone who trusts in himself is a fool.

> *The one who trusts in his own heart is a fool,*
> *but the one who walks in wisdom will escape.*
> *Proverbs 28:26*

No one in his right mind desires to be a fool.

OUT OF CONTROL

*LORD, we know that people do not control their own destiny.
It is not in their power to determine what will happen to them.*
Jeremiah 10:23

TO WHAT DEGREE are we actually in control of our lives, circumstances, and destiny? As I approached the time for surgery, I remember feeling that I was going where I did not wish to go, and there was nothing I could do about it. I felt "out of control." Every day we hear of people who die in the most unexpected ways, their lives snuffed out in their prime. Who knows what a day may bring our way? That is why James wrote:

*Come now, you who say,
"Today or tomorrow we will go into this or that town
and spend a year there and do business and make a profit."
14 You do not know about tomorrow. What is your life like?
For you are a puff of smoke that appears for a short time
and then vanishes. 15 You ought to say instead,
"If the Lord is willing, then we will live and do this or that."
16 But as it is, you boast in your arrogance.
All such boasting is evil.*
James 4:13-16

We are always "out of control" to one degree or another. Sometimes it is just more apparent to us. This is why it is so important that we know and believe that Someone is in control. If we can adjust to being personally "out of control" and relax in God's loving direction of our lives, we can have peace that passes understanding in every situation. We need not fear the future, because the Lord holds it all in His hands.

Feeling out of control is a wonderful opportunity to exercise faith. When trust in God's sovereignty is absent, we try to manipulate circumstances to provide an illusion of security. The children of Israel tried to protect themselves by refusing to attack and conquer the Canaanites in order to take the land God had promised them. Did they accomplish their goal? Absolutely not! They all died in the desert without ever having obtained what God had promised. If they had relinquished control to God and simply obeyed Him, they would have preserved their lives and obtained their goal. This is one of those paradoxes of faith: we "lose" our lives by trying to protect ourselves, and we "keep" our lives by surrendering them to the Lord.

Where are we in this process of surrendering control of our lives to God? It is all about Lordship, is it not? Have we relinquished our lives to the Lord of Life, or are we still foolishly trying to direct our own affairs? Why resist the inevitable? Ultimately God will direct our paths, one way or another. Why not get on board with His plan sooner rather than later? It is a lot more fun to choose to surrender to God than to have it forced upon us. Jesus relinquished all control of His life to His heavenly Father, and, as a result, has been given all honor, power, and authority. Not a bad exchange! What might we gain by surrendering to God what already belongs to Him – our very lives?

> *As a result God exalted him and gave him*
> *the name that is above every name,*
> *10 so that at the name of Jesus every knee will bow —*
> *in heaven and on earth and under the earth —*
> *11 and every tongue confess that Jesus Christ*
> *is Lord to the glory of God the Father.*
> *Philippians 2:9-11*

LIVING ON "BORROWED TIME"

*So teach us to consider our mortality,
so that we might live wisely.
Psalm 90:12*

"BORROWED TIME" is a period of uncertainty during which an inevitable outcome is postponed or avoided. Often we live our lives as if they will never end; but, as the old saying goes, there are two things of which we can be certain in this life - death and taxes. Why do we try to avoid thinking about death? Usually we just don't like to "go there"; yet, King David actually asked God to show him the transiency of his life, and Moses tells us that we gain much wisdom from considering our own sure demise, as we covered in an earlier chapter.

We need to remind ourselves that we are living on borrowed time here on earth. Our lives are a "loan" from God for which we will one day be held accountable to pay back with interest. Our Lord expects us to do something with this thing called "life," something lasting for the Kingdom of God and something that brings increase. This earth is not our home, nor will these natural earthly bodies last forever. The earthly must pass to make way for the spiritual and eternal version of things.

*It is the same with the resurrection of the dead.
What is sown is perishable, what is raised is imperishable.
43 It is sown in dishonor, it is raised in glory;
it is sown in weakness, it is raised in power;
44 it is sown a natural body, it is raised a spiritual body.
If there is a natural body, there is also a spiritual body.
45 So also it is written, "The first man, Adam, became
a living person"; the last Adam became a life-giving spirit.*

> *46 However, the spiritual did not come first,*
> *but the natural, and then the spiritual.*
> *47 The first man is from the earth, made of dust;*
> *the second man is from heaven.*
> *48 Like the one made of dust, so too are those made of dust,*
> *and like the one from heaven, so too those who are heavenly.*
> *49 And just as we have borne the image of the man of dust,*
> *let us also bear the image of the man of heaven.*
> *50 Now this is what I am saying, brothers and sisters:*
> *Flesh and blood cannot inherit the kingdom of God,*
> *nor does the perishable inherit the imperishable.*
> *51 Listen, I will tell you a mystery:*
> *We will not all sleep, but we will all be changed —*
> *52 in a moment, in the blinking of an eye, at the last trumpet.*
> *For the trumpet will sound,*
> *and the dead will be raised imperishable,*
> *and we will be changed.*
> *53 For this perishable body must put on the imperishable,*
> *and this mortal body must put on immortality.*
> *54 Now when this perishable puts on the imperishable,*
> *and this mortal puts on immortality,*
> *then the saying that is written will happen,*
> *"Death has been swallowed up in victory."*
> *55 "Where, O death, is your victory?*
> *Where, O death, is your sting?"*
> *1 Corinthians 15:42-55*

God wants us to hold loosely to our natural lives, always being ready to give them back to Him at a moment's notice. I remember taking my children to McDonald's when they were very young. I would buy French fries for them and afterward ask if I could have one. Not surprisingly they were reluctant to part with even one of their precious fries, even though they came from my generosity. We often act that way with God. He gives us life, but we hold onto it like Gollum clutching the ring in Lord of the Rings, murmuring, "My precious." His greediness was quintessentially ugly, and so is our clutching to these temporary lives entrusted to us by a loving Creator.

God has numbered our days, and they will continue until His plan for us here on earth ends. Afterward He will welcome us to our new home in heaven. That will be the glorious climax of this sometimes dark and often very challenging thing called life here on earth. What could be finer? Yet we often choose not to think about it! How foolish it is to live as if this life will never end! Instead we should deliberately live here on earth in the continual shadow of eternity so that we can more easily make the proper decisions and choices along the way. We cannot afford to live our earthly lives as if they were the most important thing. We cannot afford to seek security here at the expense of glory and reward in eternity. We live on borrowed time, and we need to start acting like it.

SNATCH PROOF

*My sheep listen to my voice,
and I know them, and they follow me.
28 I give them eternal life, and they will never perish;
no one will snatch them from my hand.
29 My Father, who has given them to me, is greater than all,
and no one can snatch them from my Father's hand.
30 The Father and I are one."
John 10:27-30*

IT IS IMPORTANT that we get something straight about our salvation in Christ. We are not "on our own" after having been granted forgiveness. Nor will God one day place us on a scale to see if we "measure up." Some people think that our time here on earth after becoming a believer is an extended trial period in which God tests us to see if we will prove faithful to His commands and earn heaven or not. In other words, under this concept of what it means to be "saved," we are not really saved at all. Instead, we only get a second chance at making a proper performance with more help this time. But if this is true, we are still "under the Law" and our salvation is still based on our own works, and we are still lost, since no one can ever measure up.

This is the clear lesson of Romans chapter seven. Saving ourselves is a hopeless situation at best, even for the believer.

*But if I do what I don't want,
I agree that the law is good.
17 But now it is no longer me doing it,
but sin that lives in me.
18 For I know that nothing good lives in me,
that is, in my flesh. For I want to do the good,*

> *but I cannot do it.*
> *19 For I do not do the good I want,*
> *but I do the very evil I do not want!*
> *20 Now if I do what I do not want,*
> *it is no longer me doing it but sin that lives in me.*
> *Romans 7:16-20*

If we find ourselves in this situation (and all of us do at some point, if not all the time, during our journey with God), we need a radical transformation in our thinking. The Greek word, metanoeo, is translated "to repent" in our Bibles, but it literally means "to change your mind." Salvation under the New Covenant is not a matter of our performance, but all about what or who we trust from the heart. Trusting in our own abilities has been tried for centuries and has never worked yet, nor will it ever work for us because we are hopelessly flawed at the core of our beings. We have a sin nature which by default will always incline us to do the wrong thing. The sin nature, or the "flesh," will never be reformed or rehabilitated. It is an outlaw (outside of the Law) who will betray you in a heartbeat.

God had to send Jesus, the only Person who actually could and did keep the righteous requirements of the Law, to be our substitute, to keep the Law in our behalf. Jesus lived a perfectly obedient life, and through the miracle of identification, we share in the rewards of His obedience. God placed our hopeless sinfulness upon Him and in exchange gave us Christ's perfect righteousness.

> *God made the one who did not know sin to be sin for us,*
> *so that in him we would become the righteousness of God.*
> *2 Corinthians 5:21*

Our righteousness is based on Christ's performance, not our own. Our righteousness, therefore, is not our own: it is Christ's, but it has become our own through our being identified with our Lord. We are actually in Christ, and He is in us via the Person of the Holy Spirit.

> *Then I will ask the Father,*
> *and he will give you another Advocate*
> *to be with you forever —*

> *17 the Spirit of truth, whom the world cannot accept,*
> *because it does not see him or know him.*
> *But you know him, because he resides with you*
> *and will be in you.*
> *18 "I will not abandon you as orphans,*
> *I will come to you.*
> *19 In a little while the world will not see me any longer,*
> *but you will see me;*
> *because I live, you will live too.*
> *20 You will know at that time that I am in my Father*
> *and you are in me and I am in you.*
> *John 14:16-20*

Those of us who have accepted Christ's perfect righteousness no longer need to fear being weighed in the scales of God's holy justice. On the cross, our Lord Jesus Christ took the punishment for our not measuring up to God's righteousness. As our substitute, He suffered the judgment we deserved, and it is common knowledge that, once proven innocent, a person cannot be tried again for the same crime. Likewise, once a bill has been paid on our behalf, we no longer owe it. Justification means that God has declared us to be innocent in His heavenly courtroom! Our standing with God is settled and sure. Our debt has been paid once and for all!

> *And every priest stands day after day*
> *serving and offering the same sacrifices again and again —*
> *sacrifices that can never take away sins.*
> *12 But when this priest had offered one sacrifice for sins*
> *for all time, he sat down at the right hand of God,*
> *13 where he is now waiting until his enemies are made a*
> *footstool for his feet. 14 For by one offering he has perfected*
> *for all time those who are made holy.*
> *15 And the Holy Spirit also witnesses to us,*
> *for after saying, 16 "This is the covenant that I will*
> *establish with them after those days, says the Lord.*
> *I will put my laws on their hearts*
> *and I will inscribe them on their minds,"*
> *17 then he says, "Their sins and their lawless deeds*
> *I will remember no longer."*

> *18 Now where there is forgiveness of these,*
> *there is no longer any offering for sin.*
> *Hebrews 10:11-18*

Nevertheless, obedience is still vitally important and required for Christians, but not in order to obtain a right standing before God. Instead obedience is the fruit, proof, or the result of our receiving new life and imparted righteousness. If we have been born again and the Holy Spirit lives inside us, God is at work in us so that we will want to obey God from our hearts, even though we still have a sin nature that constantly resists the things of the Spirit.

> *For I delight in the law of God in my inner being.*
> *23 But I see a different law in my members*
> *waging war against the law of my mind*
> *and making me captive to the law of sin that is in my members.*
> *Romans 7:22-23*

A battle rages inside each of us believers. (This would be a great time to read and meditate on Romans chapter seven and Galatians chapter five.) Life gives us opportunities to experience the power of God's grace to overcome the power of the sin nature on a daily basis and thereby glorify God. Life is our chance to draw near to the Father's heart to experience His perfect love at such a level that we are transformed within and without.

A mature Christian is one who serves God out of appreciation and love instead of from the terror of being ultimately rejected at Judgment Day. Making the transition from the negative mentality and motivation to the new one can be an unsettling process in which one's doctrinal moorings and foundation may seem to be shaking. It can be scary if we have long trusted in the fear of encountering God's wrath to motivate us to good works. That is a very immature and incomplete motivation. According to 1 Corinthians chapter 13, anything not done out of love is worthless in light of eternity. If we do not grow up into love motivated behavior, we may be somewhat empty handed when eternal rewards are given.

In Paul's time, Roman children were turned over to pedagogues (child conductors or tutors) who supervised their moral development until puberty. These persons would accompany them with a switch in hand. If a child transgressed, the pedagogue would let him have it with the switch while repeating to him a moral maxim. Pedagogues acted as an external restraint upon bad behavior, as does the Law with its threats of condemnation and punishment. But eventually, when the child reached puberty, he was expected to have internalized what his pedagogue had taught him. Likewise, for us Christians to grow to maturity, we must transition from the external constraint of the Law to the internal motivation of the Spirit. This is the essence of the New Covenant.

> *For this is the covenant that I will establish*
> *with the house of Israel after those days, says the Lord.*
> *I will put my laws in their minds*
> *and I will inscribe them on their hearts.*
> *And I will be their God and they will be my people.*
> Hebrews 8:10

We people of the New Covenant must learn to trust in the inner power of God's Spirit to teach, motivate and enable us to live the Christ life. Sadly many of us are not convinced that God is able. If we are trusting in our own abilities to keep ourselves, we may be terrified that the Devil may ultimately pick us off or snatch us right out of God's arms, dragging us down to hell. Of course this sounds preposterous when it is put so starkly, but many of us fear that we will be ultimately lost because we know our own weakness and are aware of our many past failures. We may have no confidence in our ability to finish the race well. Well, here is the Good News: we are not supposed to have confidence in ourselves.

> *For we who worship God in the Spirit*
> *are the only ones who are truly circumcised.*
> *We put no confidence in human effort.*
> *Instead, we boast about what Christ Jesus has done for us.*
> Philippians 3:3 (NLT)

There is only One Person who deserves our confidence, and His name is Jesus. He alone can keep us, and He has placed us in the secret place of the Father's hands from which we can never be snatched away.

> *Because of this, in fact, I suffer as I do.*
> *But I am not ashamed,*
> *because I know the one in whom my faith is set*
> *and I am convinced that he is able to protect*
> *what has been entrusted to me until that day.*
> *2 Timothy 1:12*

If we have trusted Christ to be our Savior and Keeper, we need never fear being ultimately lost again. If we trust in God alone, we will be safe.

THE GOOD SHEPHERD AND THE SECRET PLACE

The LORD is my shepherd, I lack nothing.
2 He takes me to lush pastures, he leads me to refreshing water.
3 He restores my strength. He leads me down the right paths
for the sake of his reputation.
4 Even when I must walk through the darkest valley,
I fear no danger, for you are with me;
your rod and your staff reassure me.
5 You prepare a feast before me in plain sight of my enemies.
You refresh my head with oil; my cup is completely full.
6 Surely your goodness and faithfulness
will pursue me all my days,
and I will live in the LORD's house for the rest of my life.
Psalm 23:1-6

FOR THE CHRISTIAN, safety is not the absence of danger; rather, it is the presence and protection of the Lord. When God is with us, we are always safe, even though our natural lives may be in peril and our foes may surround us. King David gave us the secret of continual peace in verse four of Psalm 23: "I fear no evil, for You are with me." We carry the secret place of God's presence and protection with us wherever we go as long as the Good Shepherd accompanies us. We know from the Bible that Jesus will never leave us or forsake us; so, we must come to believe that He is always with us, even when we cannot "feel" Him or He seems far away. Faith in God's abiding presence, then, is a big key for enjoying peace and security in God's secret place.

"If you love me, you will obey my commandments.
16 Then I will ask the Father,

> *and he will give you another Advocate*
> *to be with you forever —*
> *17 the Spirit of truth, whom the world cannot accept,*
> *because it does not see him or know him.*
> *But you know him, because he resides with you and will be in you.*
> *18 "I will not abandon you as orphans, I will come to you.*
> *19 In a little while the world will not see me any longer,*
> *but you will see me;*
> *because I live, you will live too.*
> *20 You will know at that time that I am in my Father*
> *and you are in me and I am in you.*
> *21 The person who has my commandments*
> *and obeys them is the one who loves me.*
> *The one who loves me will be loved by my Father,*
> *and I will love him and will reveal myself to him."*
> *John 14:15-21*

In the secret place, we enjoy provision and rest, restoration for our souls, and direction for our lives. God comforts us and prepares a feast for us in the presence of our enemies. Unless we understand this important truth, we will miss out on an essential part of overcoming faith. God does not remove the trial, the problem, or the enemy in order to give us peace. He gives us victory in the face of our worst fears.

The first time God revealed Himself to anyone as the Lord Our Peace (Shalom) was to Gideon, just after commissioning him to pick a fight with the local idol worshippers and then go to battle against a seemingly overwhelming enemy, the Midianites (Judges 6). What a strange time to tell Gideon that God is Shalom! But not really. God delights in revealing Himself in dire situations. That is when we most need Him and when He is most able to reveal His miracle-working power. When we are about to go into a great battle, we need to encounter the Prince of Peace in a fresh new way.

Our Lord tells us to sit down and enjoy a feast in His presence, paying no heed to the enemy gathered about us and the battle that looms.

> *You prepare a feast before me in plain sight of my enemies.*
> *You refresh my head with oil; my cup is completely full.*
> *Psalm 23:5*

Why does God do this? In reality, Jesus has already conquered every enemy, including death. He wants us to enjoy that victory despite the Devil's threats. God is glorified when His people trust Him rather than take counsel from their fears. Another thing we must understand is that goodness and mercy are our continual companions.

> *Surely your goodness and faithfulness*
> *will pursue me all my days,*
> *and I will live in the LORD's house for the rest of my life.*
> *Psalm 23:6*

I picture the goodness and faithfulness of God as constant companions who travel with us wherever we go, always looking for the chance to bless us. The Hebrew word for "pursue" means to pursue, chase, or persecute. Southerners might say that God's goodness will hound us, bringing to mind the tireless pursuit of a blood hound tracking someone by their scent. We cannot escape from God's loving kindness. In every situation goodness and faithfulness will be following fast on our heels. We just need to look. And best of all, we have the promise of eternal life in God's presence. We are not to fear anything in this life, because this is not the end of the line for us. It is only the beginning. The worst the Devil can throw at us will ultimately work for our good and God's glory. All you need is faith in the Good Shepherd.

> *But I am continually with you;*
> *you hold my right hand.*
> *24 You guide me by your wise advice,*
> *and then you will lead me to a position of honor.*
> *25 Whom do I have in heaven but you?*
> *I desire no one but you on earth.*
> *26 My flesh and my heart may grow weak,*
> *but God always protects my heart and gives me stability.*
> *Psalm 73:23-26*

OUR LAST CHANCE

I tell you the solemn truth,
when you were young, you tied your clothes around you
and went wherever you wanted, but when you are old,
you will stretch out your hands, and others will tie you up
and bring you where you do not want to go."
19 (Now Jesus said this to indicate clearly
by what kind of death Peter was going to glorify God.)
After he said this, Jesus told Peter, "Follow me."
John 21:18-19

HAVE WE EVER CONSIDERED that we can glorify God in the way that we die? How we approach and go through death will be our last testimony of God's grace here on earth. Others are watching us to see if the Lord really will be all that is needed to successfully make the transition from this life to the next. If death were always simply a matter of falling asleep and waking up in heaven, we would not need a great deal of grace. However, none of us knows what manner of death we may have to endure. Will it be painful? Will it be prolonged? Only God knows this, and Jesus is Lord over death as well as life.

When I saw him I fell down at his feet as though I were dead,
but he placed his right hand on me and said:
"Do not be afraid! I am the first and the last,
18 and the one who lives!
I was dead, but look, now I am alive —
forever and ever —
and I hold the keys of death and of Hades!
Revelation 1:17-18

God will choose what manner of death we will have to endure, just as He did for Peter. Historians report that Peter was crucified upside down, a position he chose so that he would not die exactly as did his Master. Crucifixion was a horrible way to die, but God gave him grace to endure. I remember reading the story of one of the early martyrs who was burned to death. Before going to the stake, the persecuted believer agreed with a friend that he would clap his hands if God's grace was sufficient for him during his excruciating trial. This story is found in Fox's Book of Martyrs, and here is an excerpt:

> When he had continued long in it, and his speech was taken away by violence of the flame, his skin drawn together, and his fingers consumed with the fire, so that it was thought that he was gone, suddenly and contrary to all expectation, this good man being mindful of his promise, reached up his hands burning in flames over his head to the living God, and with great rejoicings as it seemed, struck or clapped them three times together. A great shout followed this wonderful circumstance, and then this blessed martyr of Christ, sinking down in the fire, gave up his spirit,
> June 10, 1555.
> Fox's Book of Martyrs

What kind of death awaits us? Most of us do not know, but what we can be certain of is that God's grace will always be sufficient. Corrie Ten Boom was a Dutch woman from Haarlem, Netherlands, whose family helped Jews escape from the Nazis during World War II. The Ten Boom family was betrayed by a neighbor, and Corrie was sent to a concentration camp. She was miraculously released and later in life shared of what she had learned through that experience. In a letter she wrote in 1974, entitled "The World Is Deathly Ill," Corrie related how when she was young, she confided to her father that she was afraid that she would not have enough strength to die as a martyr for Christ if need be. Her kind and wise father reminded her that he gave her the money to purchase her train ticket to Amsterdam immediately before she needed it, not weeks before. He then told her that God would give her the grace to die at the time it was needed. We must have such a childlike confidence in our Lord, too.

How we die will either glorify God or make people question the reality of the gospel. The way we die will either encourage the living or make them wonder if God's grace is really enough at the time of death. Fear is perhaps the greatest enemy we may face at death - fear of judgment, fear of pain, fear of rejection, fear of being alone, fear of the unknown, fear for the welfare of those we leave behind, fear of change... the list goes on. Confidence in God's faithfulness as our Keeper provides a peace that nothing is able to overcome, not even the fear of death.

Peace I leave with you; my peace I give to you;
I do not give it to you as the world does.
Do not let your hearts be distressed or lacking in courage.
John 14:27

We have a choice to make when we confront our fears: will we "let" our hearts grow fearful and troubled or will we choose to trust the Lord. Choosing to trust God means we must erect a barrier against meditating on fearful thoughts. Instead we must choose to think on things that build faith. We must expectantly look forward to the grace that will be given to us as we need it.

Blessed be the God and Father of our Lord Jesus Christ!
By his great mercy he gave us new birth into a living hope
through the resurrection of Jesus Christ from the dead,
4 that is, into an inheritance
imperishable, undefiled, and unfading.
It is reserved in heaven for you,
5 who by God's power are protected through faith
for a salvation ready to be revealed in the last time.
6 This brings you great joy,
although you may have to suffer
for a short time in various trials.
7 Such trials show the proven character of your faith,
which is much more valuable than gold —
gold that is tested by fire, even though it is passing away —
and will bring praise and glory and honor
when Jesus Christ is revealed.
1 Peter 1:3-7

God will keep us by His grace and power until His great salvation is fully revealed at the resurrection. Until then we must make the choice to trust Him with all our hearts, knowing that His keeping power is sufficient for any and every circumstance we may face in life and at death. If we have not glorified God as much as we could have in this life, at least in death we will have a last opportunity. Let us make the most of it when our time comes. When we get to heaven, perhaps we can share our death experience testimonies with each other.

THE GREATEST THING
AND OUR FINAL DESTINATION

For this reason I kneel before the Father,
15 from whom every family in heaven and on the earth is named.
16 I pray that according to the wealth of his glory
he may grant you to be strengthened with power
through his Spirit in the inner person,
17 that Christ may dwell in your hearts through faith, so that,
because you have been rooted and grounded in love,
18 you may be able to comprehend with all the saints what is
the breadth and length and height and depth,
19 and thus to know the love of Christ that surpasses knowledge,
so that you may be filled up to all the fullness of God.
Ephesians 3:14-19

THE GREATEST THING OF ALL IS LOVE. God is love. Love is the only thing that will remain when all is said and done. Apparently, we won't need faith and hope any longer in heaven because we will be in the manifest presence of God.

And now these three remain: faith, hope, and love.
But the greatest of these is love.
1 Corinthians 13:13

God is One God, but consists of three distinct Persons, all of Whom fully love us. Jesus made it clear, however, that the Father is greater than He in honor.

My Father, who has given them to me, is greater than all,
and no one can snatch them from my Father's hand.

30 The Father and I are one."
John 10:29-30

Jesus came to the earth to reveal the Father's love to human beings and to give Himself as an act of sacrificial love in order to accomplish something marvelous - to reconcile us to His Wonderfully Great and Loving Father, Abba. Prior to His death on the cross, Jesus was excited about the prospect of being restored to intimate continual fellowship with His Abba. His anticipation of that reunion gave Him strength and courage to endure the cross.

Peace I leave with you; my peace I give to you;
I do not give it to you as the world does.
Do not let your hearts be distressed or lacking in courage.
28 You heard me say to you, 'I am going away and
I am coming back to you.' If you loved me,
you would be glad that I am going to the Father,
because the Father is greater than I am.
29 I have told you now before it happens,
so that when it happens you may believe.
John 14:27-29

Therefore, since we are surrounded
by such a great cloud of witnesses,
we must get rid of every weight
and the sin that clings so closely,
and run with endurance the race set out for us,
2 keeping our eyes fixed on Jesus,
the pioneer and perfecter of our faith.
For the joy set out for him he endured the cross,
disregarding its shame, and has taken his seat
at the right hand of the throne of God.
Hebrews 12:1-2

Jesus came to reunite us with Abba, the One Who defines love. Father God is the most loving, kind, and faithful Person we will ever have the pleasure of knowing. Knowing Him and His love on an ever expanding and deepening basis is the greatest thing and our final destination. Everything else that vies for our hearts is a worthless substitute by comparison. Nothing else is worth the effort of what we call "life." When our time comes to die, if we have not made knowing God our highest priority, we will have missed the mark.

So what do we do with this bit of information? Simply this, we must view every circumstance we face as another opportunity to grow in our knowledge of Father God and His love. His loving sovereignty will not allow anything to enter our experience that does not have the potential of drawing us into a greater revelation of Who He is and how much He loves us. In trying circumstances, we may find ourselves thinking, "Well, what if something evil happens to me or someone I love? How does that provide an opportunity to know God and His love better?" There is no adequate human answer to that question, but that is no reason for us to doubt what the Bible clearly teaches.

Some time or another each of us will face a crossroad. Will we believe what God's Word says, or will we rely on our own understanding of things? A successful journey to the secret place hinges on our answer to this question. We can only get there by choosing to rely on God alone. The Bible says that God is working all things together for good in our lives (Romans 8:28). All means all. We either choose to believe it because God says so, or we don't. If we believe that promise, we will be looking for God to reveal Himself in every situation. Jesus promised us that when we seek for God, we will find Him. It really could not be simpler.

God uses difficult things in life to break down our resistance, rebellion, fears, and stubbornness. Brokenness and surrender are of great value to God.

The godly cry out and the LORD hears;
he saves them from all their troubles.
18 The LORD is near the brokenhearted;
he delivers those who are discouraged.
19 The godly face many dangers, but the LORD
saves them from each one of them.
Psalm 34:17-19

Only a broken person can look heavenward in the midst of a severe trial and proclaim an indomitable trust in the love and wisdom of the Sovereign God who allowed such a thing to come into her life. Such a worshipful declaration is perhaps one of the greatest acts of faith a person can make. When we praise God during good times it pleases God; but, when we do so when everything seems to be against us, it brings Him great pleasure and glory. Such praise defeats the enemy and glorifies the Savior. Such faith provides an abundant entrance into the secret place of God's presence, our final destination.

The journey to the secret place is the way to find a little piece of heaven in an otherwise difficult world. Abiding in the secret place allows us to enjoy the benefits of God's presence while we wait for the day

> *"when he comes to be glorified among his saints*
> *and admired on that day among all who have believed…"*
> 2 Thessalonians 1:10